Farm Fun
Crafts for Kids

Includes Projects for Children from Preschool to Sixth Grade:

❖ **Colorful Projects with a Farming Theme**

❖ **Awards and Certificates**

❖ **Bible Memory Verse Coloring Pages**

Compiled by Heather Kempton

Blue Ribbon

Jaelen memorized all the Bible Memory Verses at SonHarvest County Fair.

Jesus Said, "My command is this: Love each other as I have loved you." John 15:12

Gospel Light

How to Make Clean Copies from This Book

You may make copies of portions of this book with a clean conscience if

• you (or someone in your organization) are the original purchaser;

• you are using the copies you make for a noncommercial purpose (such as teaching or promoting your ministry) within your church or organization;

• you follow the instructions provided in this book.

However, it is ILLEGAL for you to make copies if

• you are using the material to promote, advertise or sell a product or service other than for ministry fund-raising;

• you are using the material in or on a product for sale; or

• you or your organization are not the original purchaser of this book.

By following these guidelines you help us keep our products affordable.

Thank you,

Gospel Light

Founder, Henrietta Mears • **Publisher Emeritus,** William T. Greig • **Publisher, Children's Curriculum and Resources,** Lynnette Pennings, M.A. • **Senior Consulting Publisher,** Dr. Elmer L. Towns • **Managing Editor,** Sheryl Haystead • **Senior Editor,** Kim Fiano • **Senior Consulting Editors,** Wesley Haystead, M.S.Ed., Christy Weir • **Senior Editor, Biblical and Theological Issues,** Bayard Taylor, M.Div. • **Associate Editor,** Heather Kempton • **Contributing Writers,** Linda Crisp, Carol Eide, Neva Felino, Dianne Rowell • **Contributing Editors,** Suzanne Bass, Linda Crisp, Carol Eide, Rachel Hong, Karen McGraw, Barbara Morris, Loreen Roberts, Ellen Unseth • **Senior Designer,** Carolyn Thomas • **Illustrator,** Chizuko Yasuda • **Cover Design,** Kevin Parks

Contents

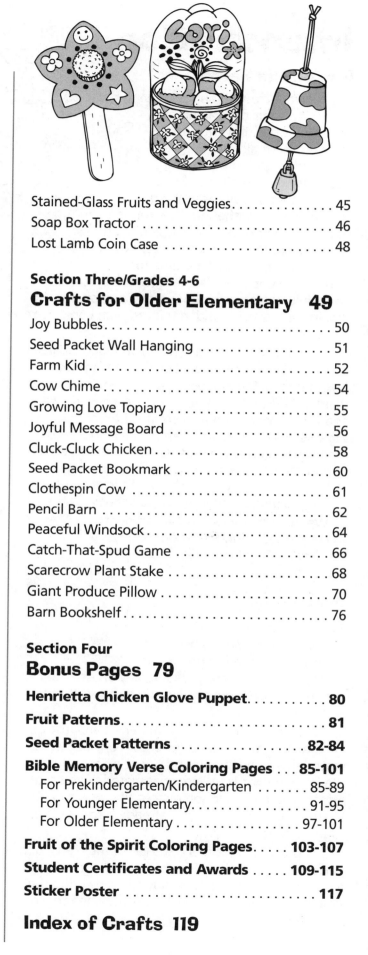

Introduction

Fun on the Farm!

The rooster's crowing and it's time to get crackin'! It's fair time again and the farm is buzzing with excitement. Folks of all ages are getting ready—growing, making and presenting their very best. The cows are ready for milking, the eggs need gathering, the fruit is ripe for the picking—and those biscuits aren't going to bake themselves! When the day is done, there'll be time for a farm-fresh supper and some down-to-earth fun. Your children can experience that atmosphere with the arts and crafts found in this resource book, *Farm Fun Crafts for Kids.*

As your children create their own works of art and learn about life on a farm, they'll learn that God's Spirit will help them to grow good fruit in their lives—fruit such as love, joy, peace, patience and kindness. As children create their crafts together, look for times to affirm that God loves them so much that He sent His Son, Jesus, to Earth so that they can become members of His family. Talk about the ways God shows His love to us. Give them opportunities to ask questions.

We hope that you and your students will enjoy many fun-filled hours creating these projects from *Farm Fun Crafts for Kids.*

Personalize It!

We encourage you to use *Farm Fun Crafts for Kids* as a basis for your craft program. You, as the teacher, parent or craft leader, play an essential role in leading enjoyable and successful craft projects for your children.

Feel free to alter the craft materials and instructions to suit your children's needs. Consider what materials you have on hand, what materials are available in your area and what materials you can afford to purchase. In some cases, you may be able to substitute materials you already have for the suggested craft supplies.

In addition, don't feel confined to the crafts in a particular age-level section. You may want to adapt a craft for younger or older age levels by using the simplification or enrichment ideas provided for certain crafts.

Three Steps to Success

What can you do to make sure craft time is successful and fun for your children? First, encourage creativity in each child! Remember, the process of creating is more important than the final product. Provide a variety of materials with which children may work. Allow children to make choices on their own. Don't expect every child's project to turn out the same. Don't insist that children "stay inside the lines."

Second, choose projects that are appropriate for the skill level of your children. Children become easily discouraged when a project is too difficult for them. Keep your children's skill levels in mind when choosing craft projects. Finding the right projects for your children will increase the likelihood that all will be successful and satisfied with their finished products.

Finally, show an interest in the unique way each child approaches a project. Affirm the choices he or she has made. Treat each child's final product as a masterpiece!

The comments you give a child today can affect the way he or she views art in the future, so make it positive! Remember, the ability to create is part of being made in the image of God, the ultimate creator!

Craft Symbols

Many of the craft projects in *Farm Fun Crafts for Kids* are appropriate for more than one age level. Next to the title of certain projects in this book, you'll find the symbol shown below. This symbol tells which projects are suitable or adaptable for all elementary-age children—first through sixth grades. As you select projects, consider the particular children you are working with. Feel free to use your own ideas to make projects simpler or more difficult depending on the needs of your children.

In addition, some craft projects in this book require less preparation than others. The symbol shown below tells which projects require minimal preparation.

suitable for all ages

minimal preparation

Be Prepared

If you are planning to use crafts with a child at home, here are three helpful tips:

❖ Focus on the crafts in the book designated for your child's age, but don't ignore projects that are listed for older or younger ages. Elementary-age children enjoy many of the projects geared for preschool and kindergarten children. And younger children are always interested in doing "big kid" things. Just plan on working along with the child, helping with tasks the child can't handle alone.

❖ Start with projects that call for materials you have around the house. Make a list of the items you do not have that are needed for projects you think your child will enjoy. Plan to gather those supplies in one expedition.

❖ If certain materials seem too difficult to obtain, a little thought can usually lead to appropriate substitutions. Often the homemade version ends up being an improvement over the original plan.

If you are planning to lead a group of children in doing craft projects, keep these hints in mind:

❖ Choose projects that will allow children to work with a variety of materials.

❖ Make your selection of all projects far enough in advance to allow time to gather all needed supplies in one coordinated effort. Many projects use some of the same items.

❖ Make up a sample of each project to be sure the directions are fully understood and potential problems can be avoided. **You may want to adapt some projects by simplifying procedures or varying the materials required.**

❖ Many items can be acquired as donations from people or businesses if you plan ahead and make your needs known. Many churches distribute lists of materials needed to their congregations and communities and are able to provide craft supplies at little or no cost. Some items can be brought by the children themselves.

❖ In making your supply list, distinguish between items that each individual child will need and those that will be shared among a group.

❖ Keep in mind that some materials may be shared among more than one age level, but this works only if there is good coordination between the groups. It is extremely frustrating to a teacher to expect to have scissors, only to discover another group is using them. Basic supplies that are used repeatedly in craft projects, such as glue, scissors, markers, etc., should usually be provided to every group.

Crafts with a Message

Many of the projects in *Farm Fun Crafts for Kids* can easily become crafts with a message. Children can create slogans or poetry as part of their projects; or you may want to provide photocopies of an appropriate poem, thought or Bible verse for children to attach to their crafts. To the right are some examples of ways to use verses and drawings to enhance the craft projects in this book.

The Farm Report

Each craft in this book includes The Farm Report, a section designed to help you enhance craft times with thought-provoking conversation that is age appropriate. The Farm Report for a project may relate to ways to grow in the fruit of God's Spirit, a Scripture verse or a Bible story related to the craft. Often The Farm Report includes interesting facts about life on a farm. If your craft program includes large groups of children, you may want to share these conversation suggestions with each helper who can, in turn, use them with individuals or small groups.

Helpful Hints

Using Glue with Young Children

Since preschoolers have difficulty using glue bottles effectively, you may want to try one of the following procedures. Purchase glue in large containers (up to one gallon size).

a. Pour small amounts of glue into several shallow containers (such as margarine tubs or the bottoms of soda bottles).

b. Dilute glue by mixing a little water into each container.

c. Have children use paintbrushes to spread glue on their projects.

OR

a. Pour a small amount of glue into a plastic margarine tub.

b. Give each child a cotton swab. The child dips the cotton swab into the glue and rubs glue on project.

c. Pour excess glue back into the large container at the end of each session.

glue level   swabs

Cutting with Scissors

When cutting with scissors is required for crafts, take note of the fact that some of the children in your class may be left-handed. It is very difficult for a left-handed person to cut with scissors that were designed to be used with the right hand. Have available in your classroom two or three pairs of left-handed scissors. These can be obtained from a school supply center.

If your craft involves cutting fabric, felt or ribbon, have available several pairs of fabric scissors for older children.

Using Acrylic Paints

Acrylic paints are required for several of the projects. Our suggestions:

❖ Provide smocks or old shirts for your children to wear, as acrylics may stain clothes.

❖ Acrylics can be expensive for a large group of children. To make paint go further, squeeze a small amount into a shallow container and add water until mixture has a creamy consistency. Or use water-based house paints thinned with water.

❖ Fill shallow containers with soapy water. Clean paintbrushes before switching colors and immediately after finishing project.

Section One/
Prekindergarten-Kindergarten
Crafts for Young Children

Craft projects for young children are a blend of "I wanna do it myself!" and "I need help!" Because each project is intended to come out looking like a recognizable something, it usually requires a certain amount of adult assistance—in preparing a pattern, in doing some cutting, in preselecting magazine pictures, in tying a knot, etc. But always take care to avoid robbing the child of the satisfaction of his or her own unique efforts. The adult's desire to have a nice finished project should not override the child's pleasure in experimenting with color and texture. Avoid the temptation to do the project for the child or to improve on the child's efforts.

Some of these crafts have enrichment and simplification ideas included with them. An enrichment idea provides a way to make the craft more challenging for the older child. A simplification idea helps the younger child complete the craft more successfully.

Although most projects in this book allow plenty of leeway for children to be creative, some children may become frustrated with the limitations of a structured craft. This frustration may be a signal that the child needs an opportunity to work with more basic, less structured materials: blank paper and paints, play dough or abstract collages (gluing miscellaneous shapes or objects onto surfaces such as paper, cardboard or anything else to which glue will adhere). In any task a young child undertakes, remember that *the process the child goes through is more important than the finished product.*

Berry Special Gift (10-15 MINUTES)

Materials
- ❖ Berry Patterns
- ❖ bright pink or red card stock
- ❖ green card stock
- ❖ white yarn
- ❖ black crayons

For each child—
- ❖ large paper clip
- ❖ two lollipops

Standard Supplies
- ❖ scissors
- ❖ measuring stick
- ❖ transparent tape
- ❖ glue
- ❖ hole punch

Preparation
Photocopy Berry and Berry Back Patterns onto pink or red card stock; photocopy Leaf Pattern onto green card stock. Make one copy of each for each child and cut out. Cut one 2-foot (.6-m) length of yarn for each child. Tie a knot about 8 inches (20.5 cm) from one end of each yarn length. Wrap tape around other end of each yarn length to make a "needle."

Instruct each child in the following procedures:

- Glue leaf onto top of berry.
- Teacher paper clips berry and berry back together and then punches holes around sides and bottom of berry (sketch a).
- Starting at one corner, thread yarn through holes (sketch a).
- Teacher ties yarn in a bow around stem at top of berry (sketch b). Remove paper clip.
- Use black crayons to draw strawberry seeds on front and back of berry (sketch c).
- Insert one lollipop in pocket on back of berry (sketch c). Give your Berry Special Gift to someone you love! Take the other lollipop home to eat!

Simplification Idea
For large groups, punch holes ahead of time.

Enrichment Idea
Use white card stock instead of colored card stock. Children use crayons or markers to color berry and berry top.

The Farm Report
What is a gift someone has given you, Tyler? Giving a gift is a kind thing to do. You could give your lollipop to someone you love. We show God's love when we are kind to each other!

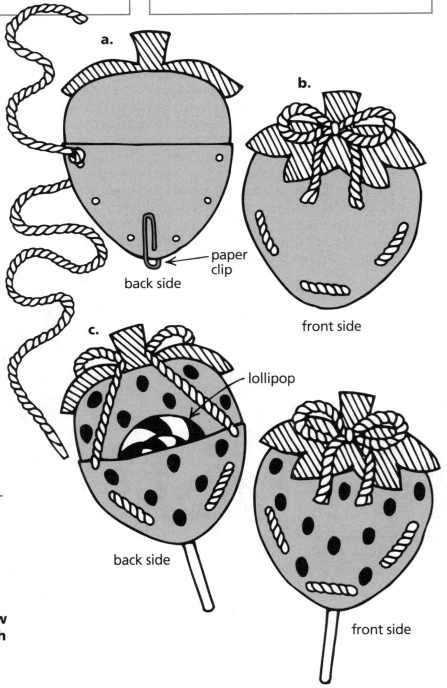

a. paper clip / back side

b. front side

c. lollipop / back side / front side

Berry Patterns

Berry

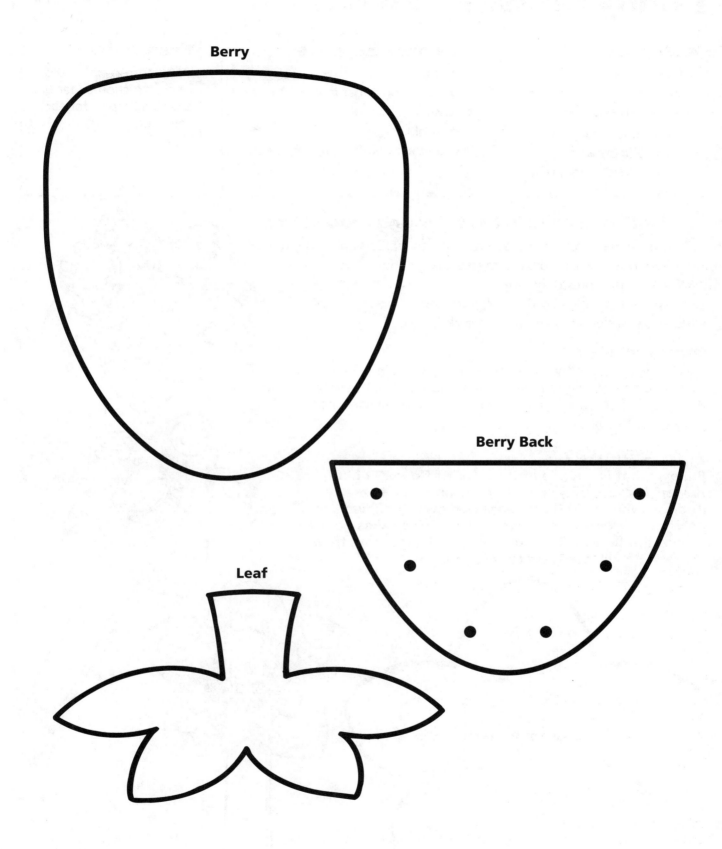

Berry Back

Leaf

Funny Flower (10-15 MINUTES)

Materials
❖ Blossom Pattern
❖ small stickers
For each child—
❖ plastic bottle cap
❖ tongue depressor
❖ 1-inch (2.5-cm) pom-pom

Standard Supplies
❖ pencil
❖ construction paper in various colors
❖ scissors
❖ craft glue
❖ wide-tip markers, including green

Preparation
Trace onto various colors of construction paper one Blossom Pattern for each child and cut out.

Instruct each child in the following procedures:
• Choose a paper blossom and decorate it with markers and/or stickers.
• Glue top of bottle cap to blossom (sketch a). Allow to dry.
• Color tongue depressor green.
• Glue pom-pom inside bottle cap (sketch b).
• Glue back of flower to end of craft stick (sketch b).

Enrichment Ideas
Children may cut out their own blossoms. Spray pom-poms with fragrance before children glue them to bottle caps. Use with Potted Love craft (p. 26); children insert craft stick directly into clay to stand upright.

The Farm Report
Bailey, what is your favorite color of flower? I like flowers because they smell so good and look so pretty. Andrew, what good things does God give the flowers to help them grow? (Water. Dirt. Sunlight.) **God takes good care of the flowers. But God loves YOU a lot more than flowers! He will take care of you, too.**

a.

b.

Blossom Pattern

Fruit Shaker (15-20 MINUTES)

Instruct each child in the following procedures:

- Paint back of paper plate red with a green edge (sketch a). Allow to dry.
- Fold paper plate in half to make a watermelon slice (sketch b).
- Teacher staples around open edges of watermelon, leaving a small opening.
- Place a handful of beans inside opening of watermelon.
- Teacher staples opening closed.
- Use marker to draw seeds on watermelon.

Simplification Ideas

Children use crayons or markers to color plates. Or fold and staple shakers ahead of time and have children paint only one side of fruit.

Enrichment Idea

Children paint backs of two paper plates the color of any round fruit. Draw a stem and leaves on green construction paper and cut out. Staple plates together with stem in between, leaving a small opening. Place beans inside fruit and staple closed (see Enrichment Idea sketch).

The Farm Report

What is your favorite fruit? Your favorite vegetable? God made all these foods for us to enjoy! Let's sing a song to thank Him. You can shake your Fruit Shaker to make music while we sing! To the tune of "Mary Had a Little Lamb," sing, **Thank You, God, for (apples and corn), (apples and corn), (apples and corn). Thank You, God, for (apples and corn). You take good care of me!** Repeat, substituting other foods that children mentioned.

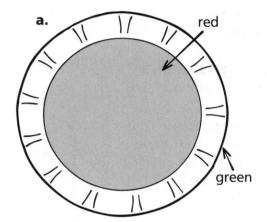

a.

red

green

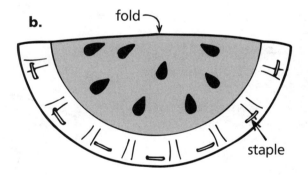

b.

fold

staple

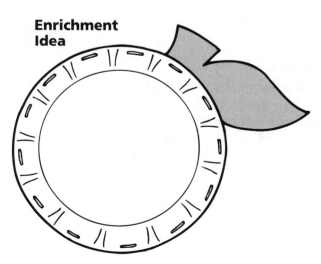

Enrichment Idea

My Own Greenhouse (15-20 MINUTES)

Materials
- Greenhouse Pattern
- stickers, rubber stamps and/or glitter-glue pens (stickers are available from Gospel Light)
- seeds (grass seed, lima beans, popcorn kernels, etc.)

For each child—
- three cotton balls
- resealable plastic sandwich bag

Standard Supplies
- white card stock
- scissors
- water
- shallow containers
- colored markers
- transparent tape

Preparation
Photocopy onto card stock one Greenhouse Pattern for each child and cut out. Cut out and discard inner portion of each frame (sketch a). Pour water into shallow containers.

Instruct each child in the following procedures:

- Use markers, stickers, stamps and/or glitter-glue pens to decorate one side of greenhouse frame. Set aside to dry.
- Dip a cotton ball in water. Pull apart wet cotton ball and place in bottom of plastic bag. Repeat with two more cotton balls.
- Sprinkle a pinch of small seeds or place several large seeds onto wet cotton balls.
- Teacher seals plastic bag and tapes to back of frame so that seeds are visible through opening (sketch b).
- At home, tape My Own Greenhouse to a window. Check each day to watch your seeds sprout and grow!

Enrichment Idea
Children cut out their own Greenhouse Patterns.

The Farm Report

Have you ever planted a seed? What happened to it? Seeds are tiny, but they can grow into great big plants. God made us, and we grow, too. Who do you know who is smaller than you? Who do you know who has grown big? God gives us strong bodies that grow.

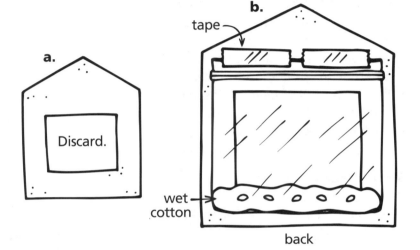

Lost Sheep Game (15-20 MINUTES)

Materials
❖ Lost Sheep Game Patterns
❖ chenille wires

For each child—
❖ two 3-ounce disposable cups (plastic or unwaxed paper)
❖ five cotton balls
❖ lunch-sized paper bag

Standard Supplies
❖ scissors
❖ white card stock
❖ crayons
❖ glue
❖ transparent tape

Preparation
Cut chenille wires in half to make one half for each child. Photocopy onto card stock one set of Lost Sheep Game Patterns for each child.

Instruct each child in the following procedures:

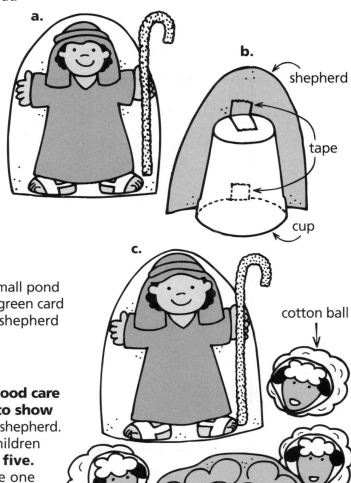

a.

b.

shepherd

tape

cup

c.

cotton ball

- Color Shepherd, Sheep and Bush Patterns and cut out.
- Bend chenille wire to make a shepherd's staff and glue to shepherd's hand (sketch a).
- With teachers help, tape shepherd and bush cutouts to sides of overturned cups so that cutouts stand up (sketch b).
- Glue one sheep cutout to each cotton ball (sketch c). Allow to dry.
- To play a simple counting game, hide one or more sheep under bush. Ask a friend to tell how many sheep are missing.
- Place all game pieces inside bag to take home.

Simplification Idea
Precut patterns for younger children.

Enrichment Ideas
Children decorate paper bags. They may also cut a small pond from blue construction paper and glue to a sheet of green card stock. Children use craft to act out the story of the shepherd who lost one sheep (Luke 15:1-7).

The Farm Report
Jesus told a story about a shepherd who took good care of his sheep. Let's use your Lost Sheep Games to show what the shepherd did. Children place sheep near shepherd. **Each night, the shepherd counted his sheep.** Children count sheep. **One . . . two . . . three . . . four . . . five. But one day, one sheep was lost!** Children hide one sheep under bush. **One . . . two . . . three . . . four—one was missing! So the shepherd searched and searched and searched!** Children walk shepherd around to look for lost sheep. **Finally, he found the sheep!** Children lift bush to reveal sheep. **The shepherd was so happy! He put the sheep on his shoulders.** Children place sheep on top of shepherd's cup. **And he carefully brought it back to the other sheep!** Children walk shepherd back to other sheep.

Lost Sheep Game Patterns

Shepherd

Bush

Sheep

Great Big Fruit (15-20 MINUTES)

Materials
- ❖ newsprint
- ❖ red, orange, peach and purple tempera paints
- ❖ green florist, electrical or masking tape

For each child—
- ❖ lunch-sized paper bag
- ❖ wired silk floral leaf (available at craft stores)

Standard Supplies
- ❖ shallow containers
- ❖ paintbrushes

Preparation
Cover work area with newsprint. Pour paints into shallow containers.

Instruct each child in the following procedures:

- Stuff bag two-thirds of the way to the top with crumpled newsprint.
- Teacher gathers top of bag and twists and wraps with tape to make a stem (sketch a).
- Paint bag to look like a fruit (apple, orange, peach or plum). Allow to dry.
- With teacher's help, wrap wire end of silk leaf to base of stem (sketch b).

Simplification Idea
Teacher stuffs bags and wraps stems in advance.

Enrichment Idea
Instead of silk leaves, children cut out leaf shapes from green construction paper and tape to fruit stems.

The Farm Report

What kinds of fruits grow on trees? (Apples. Bananas. Oranges. Plums.) **Fruit trees don't grow fruit all year. You have to wait and wait for the fruit to grow and get ripe—you have to be very patient! God wants us to be patient with other people, too. You can be patient when you're waiting for your mom to get off the phone or when you're waiting for your turn on the slide. Our Bible says, *Be patient with one another*** (see Ephesians 4:2).

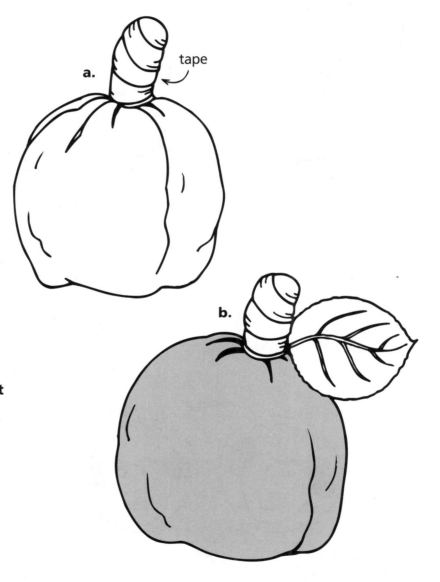

a.   tape

b.

Henrietta Chicken (15-20 MINUTES)

Materials

- ❖ Comb and Wattle Patterns
- ❖ nest-making materials (twigs, raffia, excelsior or hay)
- ❖ yellow or orange construction paper
- ❖ red construction paper

For each child—
- ❖ white paper plate

Standard Supplies

- ❖ scissors
- ❖ ruler
- ❖ transparent tape
- ❖ crayons or markers
- ❖ glue

Preparation

Cut nest-making materials into short lengths, a large handful for each child. From yellow or orange construction paper, cut one 1x2-inch (2.5x5-cm) triangular beak for each child. Trace Comb and Wattle Patterns onto red construction paper and cut one of each for each child. Cut paper plates as shown in sketch a and fold in half, creasing firmly.

Instruct each child in the following procedures:

- Tape paper beak inside fold of plate (sketch b).
- Fold plate in half along crease (sketch c).
- Draw eyes on chicken and make lines on wings for feathers.
- Glue comb and wattle to chicken's face (sketch d).
- Glue nest materials on bottom portion of chicken to make a nest (sketch d).
- Bend wings outward (sketch d).

Simplification Idea

To make this a flat craft, cut wing in one side of plate only. Children color and glue nest materials to one side of chicken only.

The Farm Report

Some farmers raise chickens and roosters. What do chickens give us for food? (Eggs.) **Every morning, farmers have to collect the eggs from the chickens' nests. We can thank God for giving us chickens, so we can have eggs to eat. What other good foods does God give us? God loves and cares for us!**

a.

Cut where indicated by dashed lines to make wings.

b.

beak

c.

d.

Comb

Wattle

Bunny's Carrot Patch (15-20 MINUTES)

Materials
- Bunny and Carrot Patterns
- brown card stock

For each child—
- one sheet blue card stock
- four craft sticks

Standard Supplies
- white card stock
- scissors
- stapler
- craft knife
- crayons, including pink, green and orange
- glue

Preparation
Photocopy onto white card stock one set of Bunny and Carrot Patterns for each child and cut out. Cut brown card stock in half lengthwise to make one long rectangle for each child; cut a wavy line along one long edge of each rectangle (sketch a). Cut four 1-inch (2.5-cm) slits in each rectangle as shown in sketch a. Staple three straight edges of each rectangle to bottom half of blue card stock sheet (sketch b).

Instruct each child in the following procedures:
- Use crayons to draw a face on bunny and color carrot tops green.
- Older children cut fringe in the wide end of each carrot top.
- Color craft sticks orange.
- Glue carrot tops to ends of orange craft sticks. Let dry.
- With teacher's help, staple bunny paws to bunny body (sketch c).
- Place carrots in slits in brown card stock. Place bunny behind brown card stock with paws hanging over front (sketch d).

The Farm Report
Some farmers grow vegetables. Why would a bunny want to have a carrot patch? Bunnies love vegetables, and their favorite is carrots. What are some things you love? Who are some people that you love? In our Bible, Jesus said, *Love each other as I have loved you* **(John 15:12). Jesus is our friend. He loves us, and He wants us to show love to others, too.**

a.
Cut four slits.
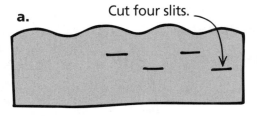

b.
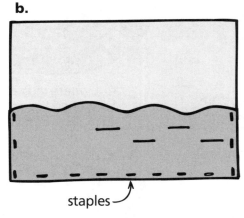
staples

c.

staple

d.

Bunny and Carrot Patterns

Bunny

Carrot Tops

Bunny Paws

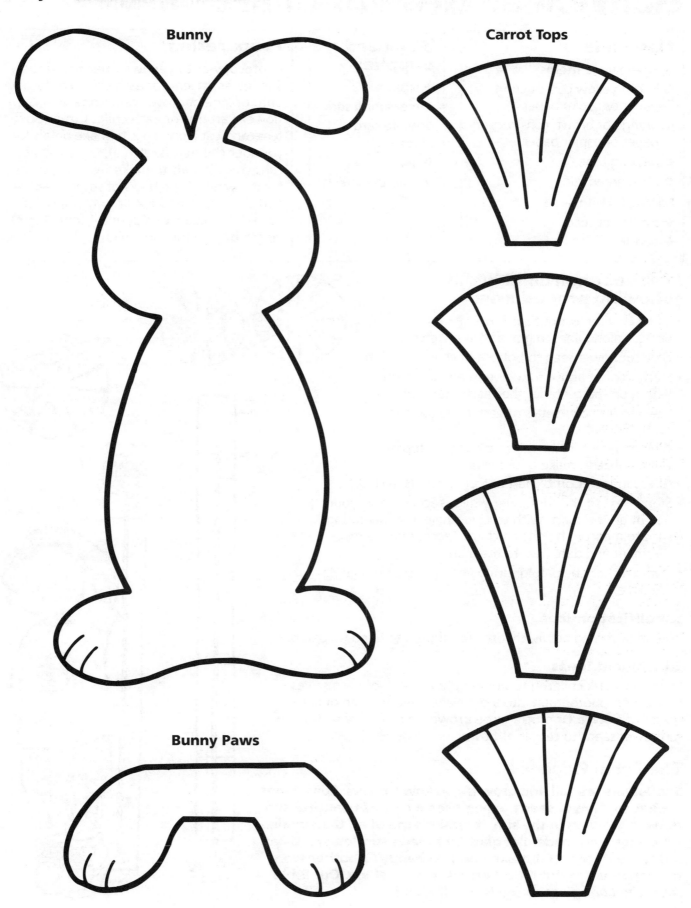

Sunflower Growth Chart (15-20 MINUTES)

Materials

❖ Sunflower Patterns
❖ bright-yellow construction paper or copier paper
❖ orange or brown construction paper or copier paper
❖ packing tape
❖ thick green yarn

For each child—

❖ sunflower seed
❖ pencil

Standard Supplies

❖ scissors
❖ measuring stick
❖ white card stock
❖ glue
❖ fine-tip marker

Preparation

Photocopy onto yellow paper one large Sunflower Pattern for each child. Photocopy onto orange or brown paper one small Sunflower Pattern for each child. Cut out patterns and cut along lines to make petals for younger children (sketch a). Cut sheets of card stock in half to make five long strips for each child. Tape backs of strips together, end to end, to make a growth chart for each child (sketch b). Cut one 4-foot (1.2-m) length of yarn for each child.

Instruct each child in the following procedures:

- Older children cut out Sunflower Patterns and cut along lines to make petals (sketch a).
- Glue sunflower seed to bottom of chart (sketch b).
- Starting right above sunflower seed, glue yarn length up the center of the chart (sketch b).
- Use pencil to curl petals of each circle toward center (sketch c).
- Glue orange or brown circle directly on top of yellow circle to make a sunflower.
- Glue sunflower onto chart at top of yarn (sketch d).
- Stand next to the sunflower while teacher marks your height on the chart. With teacher's help, use measuring stick to measure height on chart. Teacher writes measurement and date next to the mark.
- With teacher's help, fold sunflower chart accordion style (sketch e).

Simplification Idea

Instead of curling petals, children use fingers to bend up petals.

Enrichment Ideas

In advance, ask children to bring a photograph of themselves to class; cut photograph into a circle and have children glue to center of flower. Or glue a large brown pom-pom or several sunflower seeds to center of flower.

The Farm Report

Sunflowers are tall and grow big yellow flowers. Sometimes we eat sunflower seeds. When I see a row of beautiful sunflowers growing in the sun, it reminds me of all the wonderful things God made. I'm glad God made sunflowers. What are some things that make you feel happy? Another word for happy is "joyful." God wants us to feel joy. Our Bible says, *The Lord gives us joy* (see Psalm 126:3).

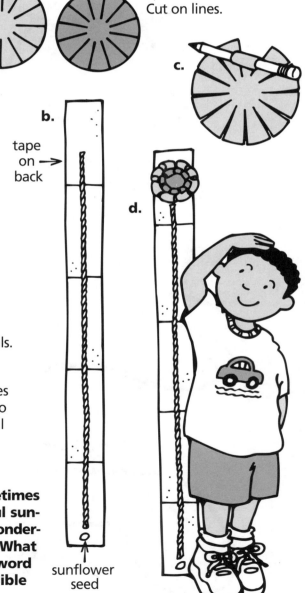

a.

Cut on lines.

c.

b.

tape on back

d.

sunflower seed

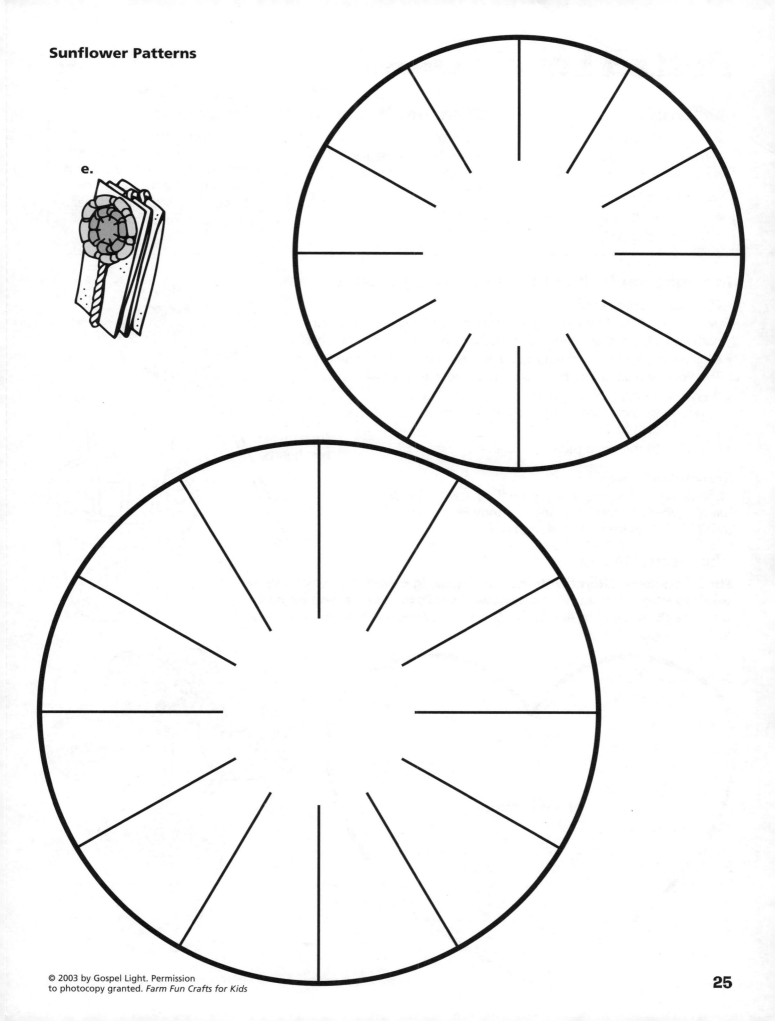

Sunflower Patterns

Potted Love (15-20 MINUTES)

Materials
❖ Heart Pattern
❖ play dough or clay
❖ shredded paper or excelsior

For each child—
❖ three chenille wires
❖ 3-inch (7.5-cm) clay pot

Standard Supplies
❖ pencil
❖ construction paper
  in various colors
❖ scissors
❖ markers
❖ glue

Preparation
Trace onto various colors of construction paper six Heart Patterns for each child and cut out. Write "Jesus loves" on sheet of construction paper for older children to copy.

Instruct each child in the following procedures:

- Choose six paper hearts.
- Write "Jesus" and "loves" on separate paper hearts. Write your name on a third heart. (Teacher writes words for younger children.)
- Glue a chenille wire to the back of each heart with a word on it. Then glue a plain paper heart on top of chenille wire (sketch a).
- Press a large lump of play dough or clay in bottom of pot. Press end of each chenille wire into dough or clay (sketch b).
- Fill pot with shredded paper or excelsior.

a.

Glue chenille wire between two hearts.

b.

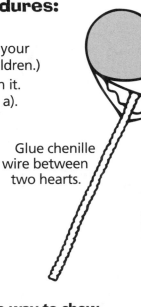

Enrichment Ideas
Children paint clay pots to decorate them (see p. 28 for painting instructions). They insert Funny Flower craft (p. 12) as well as hearts into dough or clay.

The Farm Report
Shea, you helped Hope with the glue. Helping others is a way to show God's love to them. Lucas, you showed God's love when you helped Asher with his clay. In our Bible, Jesus said, *Love each other as I have loved you* (John 15:12).

Heart Pattern

Be-Kind Ribbon (15-20 MINUTES)

Materials
- ❖ dark-blue Fun Foam or construction paper
- ❖ dark-blue tempera paint
- ❖ paint pen or glitter-glue pen

For each child—
- ❖ dessert-sized white heavy-duty paper plate
- ❖ large white lightweight paper plate

Standard Supplies
- ❖ scissors
- ❖ ruler
- ❖ newspaper
- ❖ shallow containers
- ❖ glue
- ❖ paintbrushes

Preparation
Cut two 3x9-inch (7.5x23-cm) Fun Foam or construction-paper strips for each child. Cover work area with newspaper. Pour paint into shallow containers.

Instruct each child in the following procedures:

- Paint back of smaller paper plate blue. Let dry.
- Cut slits around outside of larger paper plate, about 1 inch (2.5 cm) apart and 2 inches (5 cm) deep (sketch a).
- Glue ends of foam strips to back of larger plate (sketch b).
- Spread glue on rim of smaller plate and glue facedown to front of larger plate (sketch c).
- On front of award, teacher uses paint pen or glitter-glue pen to write "(Child's name) Is Kind."

Simplification Ideas
Omit cutting slits in large paper plate. Instead of painting, children color small paper plates with crayons or markers. Instead of Fun Foam or paper, use wide blue satin ribbon or crepe-paper streamers.

Enrichment Idea
In addition to blue, have available other colors of paint and Fun Foam or construction paper so that children can make red, purple or even rainbow-colored award ribbons.

The Farm Report
At a county fair, there are awards for lots of things. People win blue ribbons for the best animals, pies, jams and homemade clothing. Today we made blue-ribbon awards for being kind. I saw lots of you helping and sharing today. Helping other people is a kind thing to do. Our Bible says, *Be kind to each other* (1 Thessalonians 5:15).

Painted Clay Pot

(ONE OR TWO-DAY CRAFT/25-30 MINUTES TOTAL TIME)

Materials
- ❖ potting soil
- ❖ plastic dish tub
- ❖ acrylic paints in various colors
- ❖ clear acrylic spray
- ❖ large spoons
- ❖ several small watering cans filled with water

For each child—
- ❖ small clay pot
- ❖ small nursery plant

Standard Supplies
- ❖ newspaper
- ❖ shallow containers
- ❖ small paint-brushes

Preparation
Cover work area with newspaper. Pour soil into dish tub. Pour paint into shallow containers.

Instruct each child in the following procedures:

- Paint a design on your clay pot. Allow to dry.
- In a well-ventilated area, teacher sprays outside of clay pot with clear spray and allows to dry to the touch (about two minutes).
- Spoon a layer of soil into pot; then place plant in pot.
- Spoon more soil around plant to fill pot.
- Pour a small amount of water into plant.

The Farm Report

What are some things you can do to take care of your plant? (Give it water. Set it in the sun.) **Just like you can take care of your plant, God always takes care of us. One way God cares for us is by giving us people who live with us and care for us. Charlie, who takes care of you? God gives us people to take care of us because He loves us.**

Apple Harvest (20-25 MINUTES)

Material
- ❖ Apple Harvest Game Instructions (below)
- ❖ self-adhesive magnetic tape
- ❖ green construction paper
- ❖ brown craft paper or paper bags

For each child—
- ❖ small paper cup (unwaxed)
- ❖ four craft sticks
- ❖ one sheet blue card stock
- ❖ five ½-inch (1.3-cm) red pom-poms

Standard Supplies
- ❖ scissors
- ❖ ruler
- ❖ glue sticks
- ❖ glue
- ❖ stapler

Preparation
Photocopy one copy of Apple Harvest Game Instructions for each child and cut out. Cut ten ½-inch (1.3-cm) pieces of magnetic tape for each child. Cut one large treetop shape from green construction paper for each child. Cut four 1x12-inch (2.5x30.5-cm) brown-paper strips for each child.

Instruct each child in the following procedures:

- Tear each paper strip into about four shorter lengths. Use glue stick to glue them onto cup to make a basket (sketch a). Set aside to dry.
- Use glue stick to glue green treetop shape to blue card stock (sketch b). Use regular glue to glue a craft stick below the treetop to make the tree trunk.
- Peel paper backing from five magnet pieces and stick one or two to each of the remaining three craft sticks (sketch c) These will be tree branches.
- Use regular glue to glue tree branches to treetop (sketch d).
- Stick remaining magnet pieces to the five pom-poms (sketch e).
- With teacher's help, staple basket to card stock, under tree (sketch f).
- Place pom-pom apples on tree branches (sketch f).
- Use glue stick to glue Apple Harvest Game Instructions paper to back side of blue card stock.

Apple Harvest Game Instructions
Have a friend cover his or her eyes as you pick some apples off the tree and hide them in the basket. Ask your friend to tell how many apples you picked by counting how many are still on the tree.

Enrichment Ideas
Children draw leaves on tree. They stick red dot stickers on tree for extra apples. Children make additional pom-pom apples.

The Farm Report
Some farmers have lots of apple trees. It's fun to climb up in the trees and pick the apples. What foods are made from apples? (Apple pie, apple juice, applesauce, etc.) **You can pick these apples and put them in the basket. Or you can play an apple-counting game with a friend. When you take turns with a friend, you are being kind. Our Bible says,** *Be kind to each other* (1 Thessalonians 5:15).

a.

b.

c.
magnet

d.

e.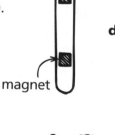

f.

Section Two/Grades 1-3
Crafts for Younger Elementary

Children in the first few years of school delight in completing craft projects. They have a handle on most of the basic skills needed, they are eager to participate, and their taste in art has usually not yet surpassed their ability to produce. In other words, they generally like what they make.

Since reading ability is not a factor in most craft projects, crafts can be a great leveler among children. Some children excel here who may not be top achievers in other areas.

You may find additional projects suitable for younger elementary children in the first section of this book—"Crafts for Young Children."

Fruity Window Cling (10-15 MINUTES)

Materials
❖ Fruit Patterns (p. 81)
❖ small squeeze bottles of white glue
❖ small mixing bowls
❖ food coloring
❖ spoon
❖ funnel

For each child—
❖ resealable plastic sandwich bag
❖ craft stick

Standard Supplies
❖ white card stock
❖ ruler
❖ scissors

Preparation
Photocopy Fruit Patterns onto white card stock, two patterns on each sheet, one pattern for each child. Then cut photocopies into 5-inch (12.5-cm) squares, with one fruit in the center of each square. Pour glue into bowls and then stir food coloring into each bowl to make purple, red, peach and green glues. Use funnel to pour each color of glue into a separate empty squeeze bottle.

Instruct each child in the following procedures:

- Choose one card-stock square and place inside plastic bag (sketch a). Leave bag unsealed.
- Set plastic bag on the table with fruit outline facing up.
- Squeeze glue over plastic bag to completely fill in fruit outline with a thick, even layer (sketch b). Use craft stick to spread glue evenly.
- Allow glue to dry overnight.
- At home, gently peel window cling off bag and stick onto window or mirror. (Hint: If window cling does not adhere, spray a fine mist of water over back side of cling before pressing onto glass.)

Simplification Idea
Purchase squeeze bottles of colored glue.

Enrichment Idea
Allow children to draw their own patterns on card-stock squares and use to make window clings.

The Farm Report
Farmers grow many, many kinds of fruit. What kind of fruit do you like to eat? Fruit helps our bodies grow healthy and strong. Besides growing healthy bodies, we can also grow good things in our lives—such as love, joy, peace, patience and kindness. The Bible calls these the fruit of the Spirit. Your Fruity Window Cling can remind you to ask God to help you grow this kind of fruit in your life.

a.

b.

32

Bottle Terrarium (15-20 MINUTES)

Materials

- ❖ gift wrapping paper in a country design (checkered, flowers, fruit, etc.)
- ❖ small disposable cups
- ❖ gravel
- ❖ potting soil
- ❖ several small watering cans filled with water
- ❖ paint pens

For each child—

- ❖ 2-liter clear plastic soda bottle
- ❖ 4-inch (10-cm)-diameter can (such as for mixed nuts)
- ❖ small nursery plant

Standard Supplies

- ❖ scissors
- ❖ pencil
- ❖ newspaper
- ❖ glue sticks

Preparation

Remove label and cut off top portion of each soda bottle (sketch a). Remove labels from cans. Using can label as a pattern, trace one rectangle onto wrapping paper for each child and cut out. Cover work area with newspaper.

Instruct each child in the following procedures:

- Glue wrapping paper around outside of can (sketch b).
- Use cup to scoop about a 1-inch (2.5-cm) layer of gravel into bottom of can.
- Scoop a layer of potting soil into can. Place plant on top of soil.
- Scoop more soil around plant to fill can.
- Place additional gravel around plant for decoration.
- Pour a small amount of water around plant. (Do not overwater, or terrarium will grow moldy.)
- Slide soda bottle over can. Use paint pens to decorate top of soda bottle (sketch d).

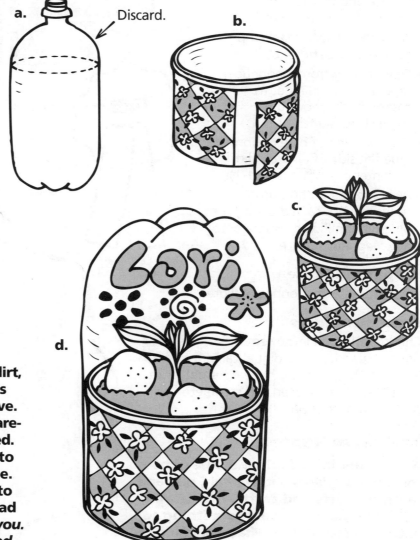

a. Discard.
b.
c.
d.

The Farm Report

A terrarium is like a tiny world with dirt, rocks, plants, air and water. Inside is everything your plants will need to live. When God made the world, He was careful to make everything we would need. He made plants and animals for us to eat, water to drink and air to breathe. Because God loves us and promises to care for us, we can have peace, instead of worry. Jesus said, *My peace I give you. . . . Do not let your hearts be troubled and do not be afraid* **(John 14:27).**

...on Picture Frame (15-20 MINUTES)

...-tip markers
...ors

For eac... ...d—
- self-adhesive magnetic tape
- juice-can lid

Standard Supplies
- lightweight cardboard
- scissors
- ruler
- craft glue

Preparation
Trace Rosette Pattern several times onto lightweight cardboard and cut out to make patterns. Cut one 5-inch (12.5-cm) square and two 1½x7-inch (4x18-cm) strips of Fun Foam for each child. Cut one 2-inch (5-cm) length of magnetic tape for each child.

Instruct each child in the following procedures:

- Trace Rosette Pattern onto foam square and cut out.
- Use markers to draw ruffles on rosette and decorate one side of each foam strip (sketch a).
- Glue end of each foam strip to back of rosette (sketch b).
- Peel backing from magnetic tape and stick magnet to rosette back, above the foam strips (sketch b).
- On front side of blue ribbon, glue flat side of juice-can lid to center of rosette (sketch c).
- At home, cut a photograph to fit inside juice-can lid. Stick your Blue-Ribbon Picture Frame onto any magnetic surface.

Simplification Idea
Precut rosettes for younger children.

Enrichment Ideas
Children glue on large sequins to give their ribbons sparkle. Use a digital camera to photograph the children; have a helper print photos so that children can complete their picture frames in class.

The Farm Report
At a county fair, people win blue ribbons for the best plants and animals, pies and jams, and arts and crafts. If you were going to make or grow something to enter in a county fair, what would it be?

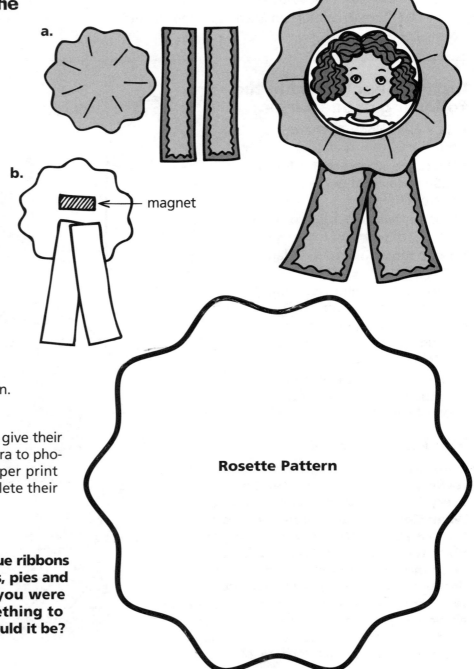

a.

b.

← magnet

c.

Rosette Pattern

Jelly Jar Ant Farm (15-20 MINUTES)

Materials
- sandy soil (or mix sand into soil)
- large bowl or shallow box
- cotton print fabric
- fabric scissors
- sponges
- large spoons or scoops
- small plastic funnels
- squeeze bottles of honey

For each child—
- large wide-mouthed plastic jar (such as for peanut butter or instant coffee)
- small wide-mouthed plastic jar that fits inside larger jar (or cut the bottom portion of an individual-sized water bottle to fit)
- plastic bottle cap
- two rubber bands

Standard Supplies
- ruler
- water

Prepara[...]
Pour soil into larg[...] bowl or shallow box. Cut one 6-inch (15-cm) square of fabric for each child. Cut sponges into squares small enough to fit in bottom of each small jar or bottle.

Instruct each child in the following procedures:

- Place small plastic jar or bottle inside large one (sketch a).
- Spoon or scoop soil through funnels to fill area between jars (sketch b). Avoid spilling too much dirt into small plastic jar.
- Wet sponge and place in bottom of small jar or bottle.
- Fill plastic bottle cap with honey and place on top of wet sponge.
- Cover top of jar with fabric and secure with two rubber bands (sketch c).
- At home, ask an adult to help you collect ants: Squeeze a long line of honey onto a sheet of paper. Leave it outside someplace where you see ants. Remove fabric from ant farm. When two or three dozen ants are on the paper, quickly drop them into ant farm and replace fabric. In a couple of days, your ants should start to build tunnels in the dirt. Add water and honey as needed.

Enrichment Ideas
Children use stickers and/or paint pens to decorate jars. Instead of having children collect ants, order them from an ant-farm supplier.

The Farm Report
It doesn't take much time to make an ant farm—but catching ants and waiting for them to build tunnels takes patience. You just can't rush an ant! What are some other fun activities that you need patience to do? (Learn to ride a bike. Make ice cream.) **We can ask God to help us be more patient.**

a.
b.
c.

). 82-84)

...ers and/or rubber
...vailable from Gospel

For ea...

❖ one or more s... envelopes, at least 3x4 inches (7.5x10 cm)

Standard Supplies

❖ white card stock
❖ scissors
❖ crayons, colored pencils or fine-tip markers

Preparation

Photocopy onto card stock several sets of Seed Packet Patterns so that there are one or more packet patterns for each child.

Instruct each child in the following procedures:

- Choose a Seed Packet Pattern and cut it out, cutting off and discarding the three tab pieces (sketch a). Fold in half along dashed center line to make a card (sketch b).
- Color card. Write a short message or draw a picture inside card, and sign your name.
- Decorate envelope with markers, stickers and/or stamps.
- Make additional cards as time allows.

Simplification Idea

Leave envelopes plain. Children take them home and address them.

Enrichment Idea

Children color cards with fruit-scented markers.

The Farm Report

Who will you give your card to? Giving a card is one way to show God's love to someone. What are some other ways we can show God's love? Jesus said, *My command is this: Love each other as I have loved you* (John 15:12).

a.

Discard.

b.

Seed Packet Plant Stake (15-20 MINUTES)

Materials
❖ Seed Packet Patterns (pp. 82-84)

For each child—
❖ bamboo skewer

Standard Supplies
❖ white card stock
❖ crayons or markers
❖ scissors
❖ craft glue
❖ hole punches

Preparation
Photocopy onto card stock several sets of Seed Packet Patterns so there is at least one packet pattern for each child.

Instruct each child in the following procedures:

• Choose a Seed Packet Pattern. Color, cut out, fold and glue pattern to make a seed packet (see pattern page sketch and sketch a here).

• Punch a hole in bottom of seed packet along the fold (sketch b).

• Put a drop of glue on dull end of bamboo skewer and insert into hole and inside of seed packet.

• At home, stick skewer into the soil of a potted plant to display your plant stake.

Enrichment Idea
Give each child a small potted flowering plant to stick their plant stakes into.

The Farm Report

Gardeners use plant stakes to remind them what kind of plant is growing in each part of their gardens. Your plant stakes show some good things that can grow in our lives if we ask God to help us. What are they? (Love, joy, peace, patience and kindness.) **The Bible calls those things the fruit of the Spirit. Your plant stakes can remind you to keep growing the fruit of the Spirit.**

front   back

a.

b.

hole

Piggy Pocket (20-25 MINUTES)

Materials

- Piggy Patterns
- light pink or peach Fun Foam
- dark pink, orange or red Fun Foam
- narrow black cording
- black permanent markers

For each child—

- large paper clip
- two 1-inch (2.5-cm) wiggle eyes

Standard Supplies

- hole punch
- scissors
- measuring stick
- craft glue

Preparation

Trace onto lighter-colored Fun Foam one Snout Pattern and two Face Patterns for each child and cut out. Through both foam face pieces, punch 16 evenly spaced holes around sides and bottom edge (sketch a). Clip a large paper clip to top edge to secure. Trace one Cheeks Pattern onto the darker-colored Fun Foam for each child and cut out. Cut one 28-inch (71-cm) length of cording for each child; tie a knot 6 inches (15 cm) from one end of each cording length.

Instruct each child in the following procedures:

- Thread long end of cording through one top hole of pocket (sketch b).
- Lace cording through holes around all edges.
- With teacher's help, tie a knot at the last hole. Tie free ends of cording together in a single knot to make handle (sketch c).
- Glue foam ears to top of pocket (sketch d).
- Glue foam cheeks near bottom of pocket (sketch d).
- Draw nostrils on foam snout. Glue snout over center of cheeks (sketch e).
- Glue wiggle eyes above snout (sketch e).

Enrichment Ideas

Trace Snout, Cheeks and Ear Patterns onto card stock and cut out several of each pattern; children trace patterns onto foam and cut out their own snouts, cheeks and ears. Children form half of a chenille wire into a loose coil and glue onto back of Piggy Pocket for a curly tail.

The Farm Report

If you had a lot of money, what would you do with it? Jesus told a story about a young man who got a lot of money and left his father's farm. He wasted his money on parties. He had to get a job feeding pigs. He was so hungry he wanted to eat the pigs' food. Finally, he went home and apologized to his father. His father forgave him and welcomed him home. God is like that father. When we are sorry for the wrong things we've done, God always forgives us.

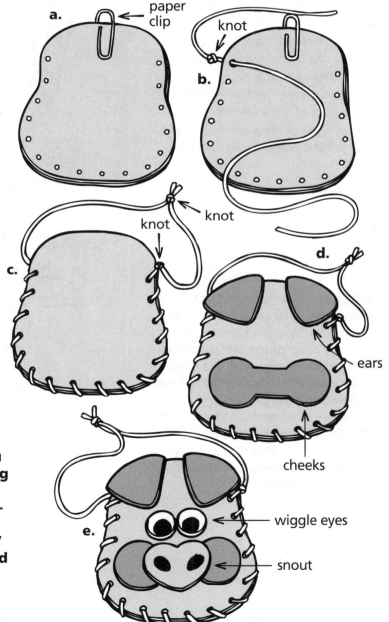

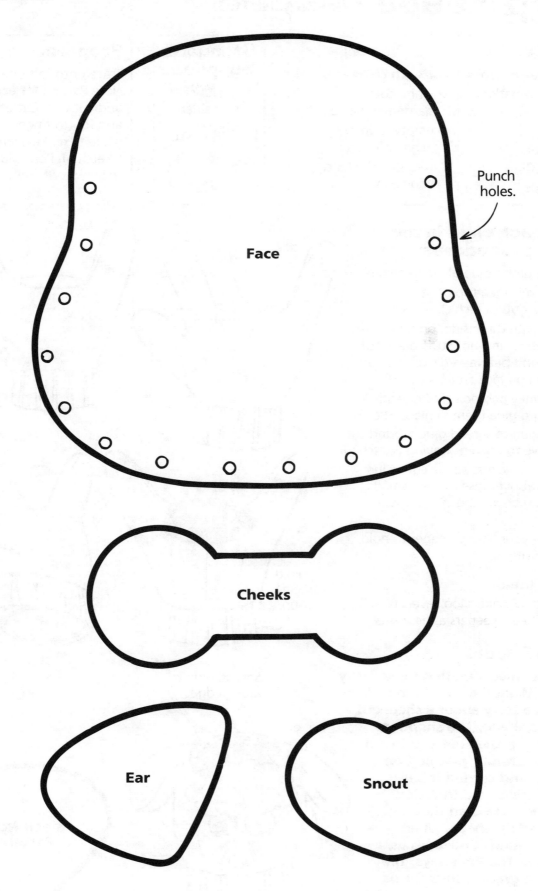

Punch holes.

Face

Cheeks

Ear

Snout

Sheep Keeper (20-25 MINUTES)

Materials

- ❖ Sheep Nose Pattern
- ❖ white fabric-marking pencil
- ❖ black felt
- ❖ fabric scissors
- ❖ fiberfill stuffing
- ❖ cotton swab

For each child—

- ❖ white cotton gardening glove
- ❖ empty soup or vegetable can
- ❖ two ½-inch (1.3-cm) wiggle eyes

Standard Supplies

- ❖ shallow containers
- ❖ craft glue

Preparation

Trace onto felt one Sheep Nose Pattern for each child and cut out. Cut off third and fourth fingers of each glove to make a large hole (sketch a). Pour glue into shallow containers.

Instruct each child in the following procedures:

- Tuck glove thumb inside glove (sketch b).
- Slide glove over open top of can. Fold glove cuff up (sketch c).
- Place glove (with can inside) on table with back of glove facing up. Stuff pieces of fiberfill stuffing between glove and can to fill out sheep's face area (sketch d).
- Fold down pinky and pointer fingers to make ears, and glue them in place (sketch e).
- Use cotton swab to spread glue around cut edges of glove to prevent fraying (sketch e).
- Glue nose to glove just above cuff. Glue wiggle eyes above nose. Glue a small ball of stuffing above the eyes for wool (sketch e).
- At home, use your Sheep Keeper to hold pens and pencils.

Enrichment Idea

Children may also make Moo Savers (p. 41) and use with Sheep Keepers as desk sets.

The Farm Report

Have you ever lost something you really cared about? What did you do to look for it? Jesus told a story about a shepherd who lost one sheep. The shepherd searched and searched until he found his sheep. He carefully placed it on his shoulders and carried it back to the flock. Jesus said that God loves us even more than that shepherd loved his sheep. When we know how much God loves us, we can feel joy. The Bible says, *The Lord has done great things for us, and we are filled with joy* (Psalm 126:3).

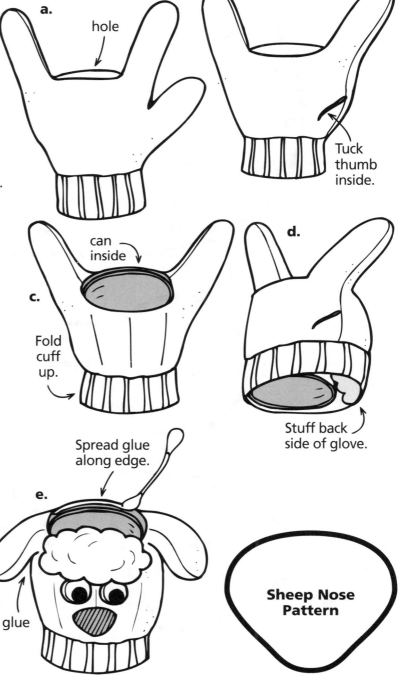

a. hole

b. Tuck thumb inside.

c. can inside — Fold cuff up.

d. Stuff back side of glove.

e. Spread glue along edge. glue

Sheep Nose Pattern

40

Moo Saver (20-25 MINUTES)

Materials

- ❖ Cow Nose Pattern
- ❖ tan felt
- ❖ black acrylic paint
- ❖ disposable plastic plates
- ❖ fiberfill stuffing
- ❖ sponges
- ❖ black permanent fine-tip markers

For each child—

- ❖ white cotton gardening glove
- ❖ empty soup or vegetable can
- ❖ two ½-inch (1.3-cm) wiggle eyes

Standard Supplies

- ❖ newspaper
- ❖ craft glue

Preparation

Trace onto felt one Cow Nose Pattern for each child and cut out. Cover work area with newspaper. Pour a small amount of paint onto each plastic plate.

Instruct each child in the following procedures:

- Tuck glove thumb inside glove (sketch a).
- Push stuffing into the tips of center two upright fingers and then push them down into glove to make 2-inch (5-cm) horns (sketch b). Push a large handful of stuffing into palm of glove.
- Slide glove over open top of can (sketch c).
- Place glove (with can inside) on table with back of glove facing up. Fold down pinky and pointer fingers to make ears and glue them in place (sketch d).
- Dab a sponge into black paint and then dab sponge onto ears and face to make spots (sketch d). Let dry.
- Use permanent marker to draw nostrils on felt nose (sketch e).
- Glue nose to glove just above cuff. Glue wiggle eyes above nose (sketch e).
- To store something inside Moo Saver at home, remove can from glove, place item inside can and place can back inside glove.

Enrichment Idea

Children may also make Sheep Keepers (p. 40) and use with Moo Savers as desk sets.

The Farm Report

What will you put inside your Moo Saver? You can use your Moo Saver to save something you don't want to lose. Jesus told a story about a woman who lost something very special to her—a silver coin. She had nine more just like it, but she still cared about that one coin—so she searched her whole house. When she found it, she was so happy! Jesus said that God is like that woman. When even one person loves Him and chooses to be in His family, God is filled with joy.

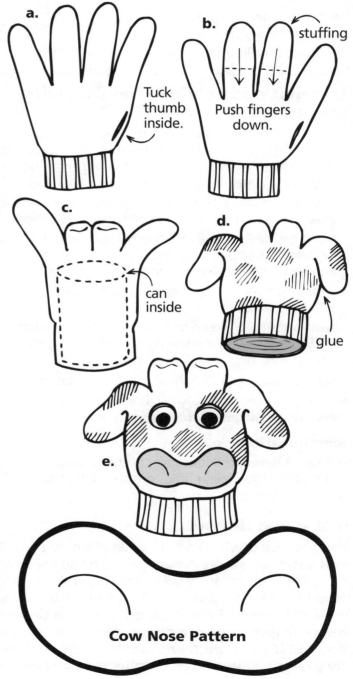

a. Tuck thumb inside.

b. stuffing Push fingers down.

c. can inside

d. glue

e.

Cow Nose Pattern

Pea Pod Catcher (25-30 MINUTES)

Materials

- ❖ cotton string
- ❖ several rolls of green electrical tape
- ❖ green tissue paper
- ❖ ⅞-inch (2.2-cm) PVC pipe
- ❖ pipe cutter or saw
- ❖ waxed paper

For each child—
- ❖ 20-ounce plastic water bottle
- ❖ 1½-inch (4-cm) Styrofoam ball
- ❖ bumpy chenille wire (any flower color)
- ❖ green chenille wire

Standard Supplies

- ❖ craft knife
- ❖ scissors
- ❖ ruler
- ❖ newspaper
- ❖ shallow containers
- ❖ water
- ❖ white glue
- ❖ large paintbrushes

Preparation

Use craft knife to cut a 2½x5-inch (6.5x12.5-cm) oval in the side of each water bottle and a small slit in the bottom of bottle (sketch a). Cut one 2-foot (.6-m) length of string for each child and insert a string into slit in each bottle. Tape string to inside bottom of each bottle to secure. Cut or tear tissue paper into 2-inch (5-cm)-wide strips, enough for each child to cover outside of water bottle. Cover work area with newspaper. Mix equal parts glue and water in shallow containers. Cut or saw one 4-inch (10-cm) length of PVC for each child.

Instruct each child in the following procedures:

- Tear tissue paper strips into 1- to 2-inch (2.5- to 5-cm) pieces. Brush bottle with glue mixture and cover with tissue pieces. Work in small sections until entire bottle is covered (sketch b). Make sure string is kept free.

- Use electrical tape to secure end of string to Styrofoam ball. Then use more tape to cover ball completely (sketch c).

- Insert end of PVC pipe into opening of water bottle. With teacher's help, wrap electrical tape around pipe and bottle neck to secure and decorate (sketch d).

- Bend and twist bumpy chenille wire to make a flower (sketch e).

- Twist one end of green chenille wire around center of flower and wrap remaining wire around bottle neck (sketch f).

- Set Pea Pod Catcher on sheet of waxed paper to dry.

- To play with Pea Pod Catcher, hold toy by handle and try to swing ball into pod opening.

Simplification Idea

Instead of having children cover bottles with green tissue paper, use green bottles or spray-paint bottles green in advance.

The Farm Report

Can you guess what part of a pea plant you eat? When you eat peas, you're actually eating the seeds of the pea plant. Peas grow inside pods. What does your craft look like? (A giant pea pod.) **The bottle is the pod, and the ball is a pea. If you plant dried peas in the ground, they will grow into pea plants. Pea plants start off tiny, but if you plant them next to a fence or a pole, they can climb up and grow taller than you are!**

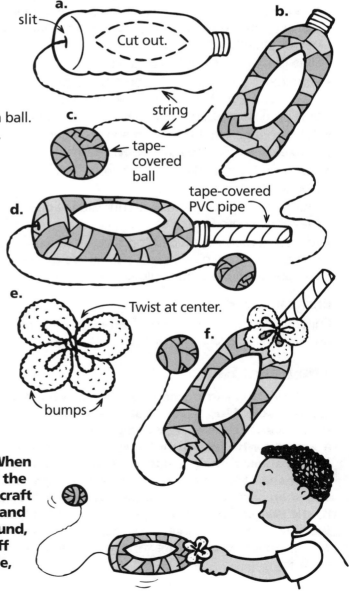

a. slit — Cut out.

b.

string

c. tape-covered ball

tape-covered PVC pipe

d.

e. Twist at center.

bumps

f.

Piggy Bank (20-25 MINUTES)

Materials

- ❖ blow-dryer
- ❖ large nail
- ❖ pink felt
- ❖ pink chenille wires
- ❖ pink acrylic paint

For each child—

- ❖ short 12-ounce plastic water bottle with cap
- ❖ four 1-inch (2.5-cm) wooden spools
- ❖ two large wiggle eyes

Standard Supplies

- ❖ craft knife
- ❖ scissors
- ❖ ruler
- ❖ newspaper
- ❖ shallow containers
- ❖ paintbrushes
- ❖ craft glue
- ❖ fine-tip markers

Preparation

Use blow-dryer to warm water-bottle labels and then peel them off. In the side of each bottle, use craft knife to cut a slot large enough for coins to be inserted; use nail to poke a small hole in the bottom near the edge (sketch a). Cut one 3-inch (7.5-cm) square of felt for each child. Cut chenille wires in half to make one half for each child. Cover work area with newspaper. Pour paint into shallow containers.

Instruct each child in the following procedures:

- Paint spools pink. Set aside to dry.
- Cut felt square in half diagonally to form two triangles. Fold triangles in half and glue together to make ears (sketch b). Set aside to dry.
- Remove cap from bottle. Trace around cap to make a circle on additional pink felt and cut out.
- Draw two nostrils on felt circle. Screw cap back on bottle and glue circle to cap to make a snout (sketch c). (Make sure slot is on top side of Piggy Bank.)
- Glue on wiggle eyes and felt ears (sketch c). (Make sure slot is on top side of Piggy Bank.)
- Curl chenille wire around marker and slide off to make a curly tail. Put a small amount of glue on end of tail and insert into hole in bottle (sketch d).
- Glue spools on bottom of pig for legs (sketch d).
- At home, use your Piggy Bank to save your coins for something special.

Enrichment Idea

Mix glue and water in a shallow container. Children brush bottle with glue mixture and then apply small pieces of pink tissue paper to cover bottle.

The Farm Report

What could you save money for in your Piggy Bank? If you are patient, you can save enough for something special. Jesus told a story about a young man who wasn't patient at all! He left his father's farm and spent all his money. The only job he could get was feeding pigs. He didn't even have enough food to eat. Finally, he went home and apologized. His very patient father forgave him. The father was so glad his son was home again! When we ask God to forgive us, He's like the father in the story— He forgives us!

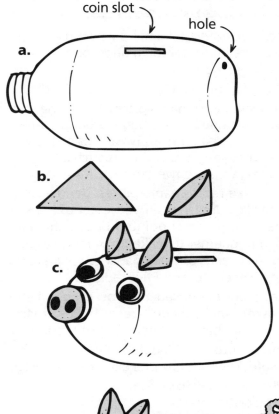

coin slot

hole

a.

b.

c.

d.

Garden Patch Tic-Tac-Toe (25-30 MINUTES)

Materials

❖ red and orange bumpy chenille wires
❖ green tissue paper
❖ solid color or small-print fabric
❖ serrated knife
❖ black permanent marker
❖ brown tempera paint

For each child—

❖ 3x4x4-inch (7.5x10x10-cm) floral foam brick
❖ plastic berry basket

Standard Supplies

❖ scissors
❖ ruler
❖ newspaper
❖ shallow containers
❖ pencils
❖ paintbrushes

Preparation

Cut chenille wire between bumps (sketch a). Cut five orange bumps and five red bumps for each child. Cut ten 1x2-inch (2.5x5-cm) tissue-paper strips for each child. Cut one 10-inch (25.5-cm) square of fabric for each child. Use serrated knife to cut narrow wedges from bottom of each foam brick so that foam fits inside strawberry basket (sketch b). On the top of each foam brick, use marker to mark nine evenly spaced dots for a Tic-Tac-Toe grid (sketch c). Cover work area with newspaper. Pour paint into shallow containers.

Instruct each child in the following procedures:

- Use a pencil to poke holes where black dots are on top of foam brick for a Tic-Tac-Toe grid.
- Paint top of foam brown to look like dirt.
- To make carrot game pieces: Wrap one end of an orange chenille bump around center of a tissue paper strip. Twist ends of tissue paper to secure carrot top (sketch d). Repeat to make five carrots.
- To make radish game pieces: Bend a red chenille bump in half over center of a tissue paper strip. Twist pointed tips of chenille bump together to make tip of radish (sketch e). Twist ends of tissue paper to secure radish top. Repeat to make five radishes.
- Lay fabric piece diagonally over top of berry basket, print side up (sketch f). Push foam brick into berry basket on top of fabric.
- Insert carrots and radishes in holes in brick. (Note: There will be one extra game piece.)
- Play Garden Patch Tic-Tac-Toe just like regular Tic-Tac-Toe.

The Farm Report

We show our love for God when we are kind to others. When we are kind, we care about what others want or need and then we help them. The Bible says, *Be kind to each other* (1 Thessalonians 5:15). **How can we be kind when we are playing Tic-Tac-Toe?** (Play with someone who is lonely. Wait patiently for your turn. Be friendly whether you win or lose. Teach a younger child how to play.)

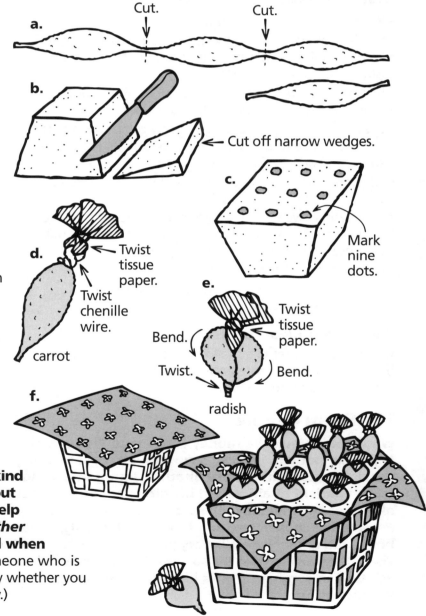

a. Cut. Cut.

b. Cut off narrow wedges.

c. Mark nine dots.

d. Twist tissue paper. Twist chenille wire. carrot

e. Bend. Twist. Bend. Twist tissue paper. radish

f.

Stained-Glass Fruits and Veggies

(25-30 MINUTES)

Materials

- ❖ Fruit Patterns (p. 81)
- ❖ premade sugar-cookie dough
- ❖ sharp knife
- ❖ aluminum foil
- ❖ hard candies in various colors
- ❖ reasealable plastic sandwich bags
- ❖ cutting board
- ❖ hammer or wooden mallet
- ❖ flour
- ❖ spoons
- ❖ permanent fine-tip marker
- ❖ cookie sheets
- ❖ oven
- ❖ oven mitt

Optional—
- ❖ Fruit of the Spirit Coloring Pages (pp. 103-107)
- ❖ crayons or colored markers

For each child—
- ❖ moist towelette

Standard Supplies

- ❖ shallow containers

Preparation

Photocopy several copies of Fruit Patterns page for children to refer to. Slice one approximately ½-inch (1.3-cm) slice of cookie dough for each child. Tear off a square of aluminum foil for each child to work on. Separate candies by color and place into separate plastic bags. Place sealed bags on cutting board and use hammer or mallet to crush candy into smaller pieces. Empty each bag into a separate shallow container. Pour flour into additional shallow containers. Place a spoon in each shallow container. Preheat oven to 350°F. (Optional: Photocopy one Fruit of the Spirit Coloring Page for each child.)

Instruct each child in the following procedures:

- Use marker to write name on foil, near the edge (sketch a).
- Use moist towelette to clean hands.
- Roll dough into a long thin rope. Add flour as necessary so that dough is not too sticky.
- Place rope on aluminum foil and shape it into the outline of a fruit or vegetable (sketch a). Refer to Fruit Patterns page if necessary. Press ends of dough together to join them.
- Fill the outline with a thin layer of crushed candy (sketch b). Use one color in each space, or blend two or more colors. Place foil on cookie sheet.
- Teacher places cookie sheet in oven. Bake cookies until candy has melted and starts to bubble (about 12 minutes). (Optional: If children will be in class during cooking time, make Fruit of the Spirit Coloring Pages available for coloring.)
- Teacher removes cookie sheet from oven and allows to cool. Carefully peel foil from back of cookie.

Enrichment Ideas

Allow children to crush the candy themselves. Before baking, press a large paper clip into top of cookie to use as a hanger.

The Farm Report

Have you ever eaten a piece of fruit that wasn't ripe yet? How did it taste? Farmers have to wait until just the right time before they pick their fruit. Farmers have to be VERY patient. The Bible says, *Be completely humble and gentle; be patient* (Ephesians 4:2).

a.   **b.** green candy

Sarah   Sarah

red candy

Soap Box Tractor

(TWO-DAY CRAFT/15-20 MINUTES EACH DAY)

Materials
- ❖ small aspirin boxes
- ❖ large nail
- ❖ black construction paper
- ❖ green and black acrylic paints
- ❖ chenille wires
- ❖ black fine-tip permanent markers

For each child—
- ❖ small rectangular bath soap box
- ❖ two large wooden wheels
- ❖ two small wooden wheels
- ❖ two ½-inch (1.3-cm) yellow or white buttons

Standard Supplies
- ❖ scissors
- ❖ ruler
- ❖ newspaper
- ❖ shallow containers
- ❖ paintbrushes
- ❖ craft glue

DAY ONE Preparation

Cut aspirin boxes in half to make one half for each child (sketch a). Cut one 2x3-inch (5x7.5-cm) construction-paper rectangle for each child. Use nail to gently poke two holes in each side of each soap box for wheel axles (sketch b). Cover work area with newspaper. Pour paints into shallow containers.

Instruct each child in the following procedures:

- Cut rectangular openings on all four sides of aspirin box for windows (sketch c). This will be the tractor cab.
- Leaving one end of soap box open, paint outsides of soap box and tractor cab green. Let dry.
- Paint wooden wheels black. Let dry.

DAY TWO Preparation

Cut chenille wires into two 4-inch (10-cm) lengths for each child.

Instruct each child in the following procedures:

- Place hand inside soap box to guide chenille wire lengths through corresponding holes in tractor base (sketch d). Glue flaps of soap box closed.
- Attach wheels to tractor base by pushing wires through holes in wheels (small wheels in front, large wheels in back). Bend ends of wires against the wheels to secure (sketch d).
- Glue closed side of cab onto top of tractor base above large wheels (sketch d).
- Make small folds on opposite ends of construction paper rectangle for the cab roof (sketch d). Glue roof onto cab, flaps facing front and back (sketch d).
- Glue buttons to front of tractor for headlights (sketch e). Use marker to draw a grill below headlights.

Simplification Ideas
Make this a one-day craft by spray-painting tractor bases, cabs and wheels before class. Cut out tractor cab windows for younger children.

The Farm Report
Who has seen a real tractor? Why do you think farmers use tractors? Tractors are very useful. Farmers use them to help dig up the dirt so that it's ready for planting, to plant seeds, and to harvest the crops when they are ready.

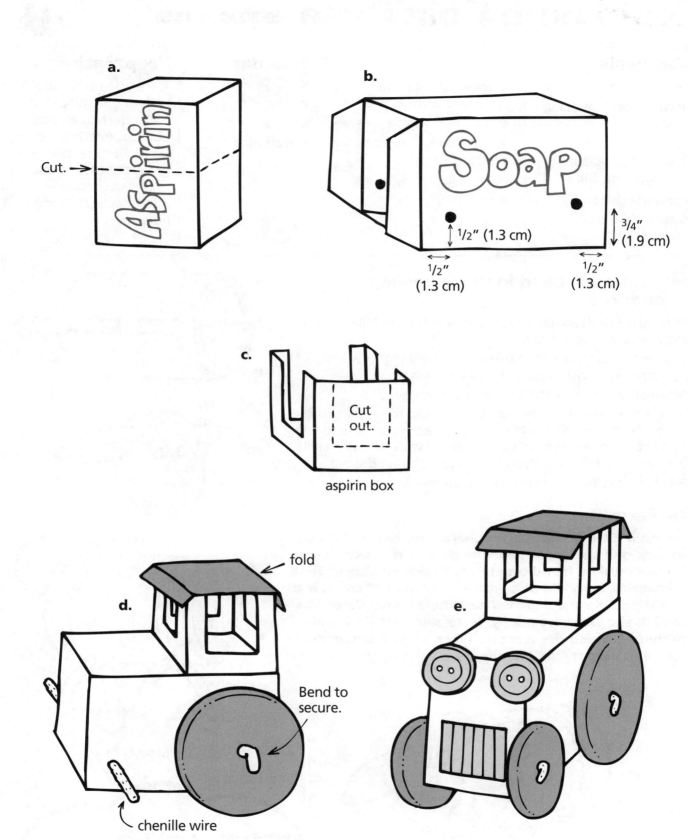

a.

Cut. →

Aspirin

b.

Soap

½″ (1.3 cm)

¾″ (1.9 cm)

½″ (1.3 cm)

½″ (1.3 cm)

c.

Cut out.

aspirin box

d.

fold

Bend to secure.

chenille wire

e.

Lost Lamb Coin Case (25-30 MINUTES)

Materials
- ❖ Lamb Face Pattern
- ❖ white fabric-marking pencil
- ❖ black felt
- ❖ white fleece fabric or synthetic fur

For each child—
- ❖ two white chenille wires
- ❖ empty 35-mm film canister with lid
- ❖ two small wiggle eyes
- ❖ 5-mm pink pom-pom
- ❖ cotton ball
- ❖ four black pony beads
- ❖ coin

Standard Supplies
- ❖ scissors
- ❖ ruler
- ❖ craft glue

Preparation
Trace one Lamb Face Pattern onto black felt for each child and cut out. Cut one 2x5-inch (5x12.5-cm) rectangle of fleece or fur for each child. Cut chenille wires into 8-inch (20.5-cm) lengths.

Instruct each child in the following procedures:

- Take lid off film canister. Glue fabric or fur around film canister (sketch a). Let dry.
- Glue felt lamb's face onto canister lid. Glue wiggle eyes and pom-pom nose onto lamb's face (sketch b).
- Glue cotton ball to bottom of film canister (sketch c).
- Wrap chenille wire around canister and twist to secure to make lamb's front legs. Place a black bead on each end of wire and bend up to secure bead (sketch c). Repeat with second chenille wire to make back legs. Adjust wires to make lamb stand.
- Place coin inside film canister and snap on lid.

The Farm Report

Jesus told a story about a shepherd who had 100 sheep. One day, one sheep got lost! The shepherd searched and searched until he found the sheep. He was so happy! Jesus told another story about a woman who had 10 coins. But she lost one! So she searched her whole house. When she found it, she was very happy. Jesus said that God is like the shepherd and the woman. When even one person becomes a part of God's family, He is full of joy!

a.

film canister

fleece or fur

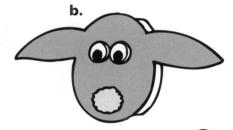

b.

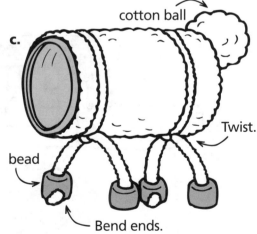

cotton ball

c.

bead

Twist.

Bend ends.

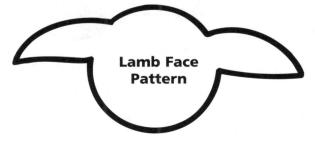

Lamb Face Pattern

Section Three/Grades 4-6
Crafts for Older Elementary

Trying to plan craft projects for older children has driven many teachers prematurely gray. The challenge is that though these children have well-developed skills to complete projects, they also have well-developed preferences about what they want to do. Sometimes a challenging project may not appeal to these young sophisticates, while a project that seems too juvenile to the adult will click with the kids!

We think you'll find projects in this section to satisfy the varied tastes of older elementary children. But a sense of humor and these tips will surely help: Filter craft ideas through a panel of experts—two or three fifth graders. If they like something, chances are the rest of the group will, too. Also, the better you get to know your students, the better your batting average will be.

Joy Bubbles (15-20 MINUTES)

Materials
- ❖ narrow satin cording
- ❖ small beads in various colors and shapes
- ❖ paint pens in various colors
- ❖ small decorative items such as stickers, pom-poms, wiggle eyes, chenille wires and Fun Foam or felt scraps

For each child—
- ❖ plastic or metal lanyard clip
- ❖ tiny bottle of bubbles (available at craft and party supply stores)

Standard Supplies
- ❖ scissors
- ❖ ruler
- ❖ craft glue

Preparation
Cut one 8-inch (20.5-cm) length of satin cording for each child.

Instruct each child in the following procedures:

- Knot middle of satin cord to lanyard clip (sketch a).
- Wrap cord around neck of bottle and double knot (sketch b).
- String several beads onto each end of cord and knot each end to secure beads (sketch c).
- Decorate bottle with paint pens and decorative items. Allow to dry.
- Clip bottle onto backpack or belt loop.

The Farm Report

What are some ways people express joy? At some parties and weddings, people blow bubbles to celebrate the joyful occasion. God has given us lots of reasons to be joyful. Psalm 126:3 says, *The Lord has done great things for us, and we are filled with joy.* What are some things God has done that make you feel joy?

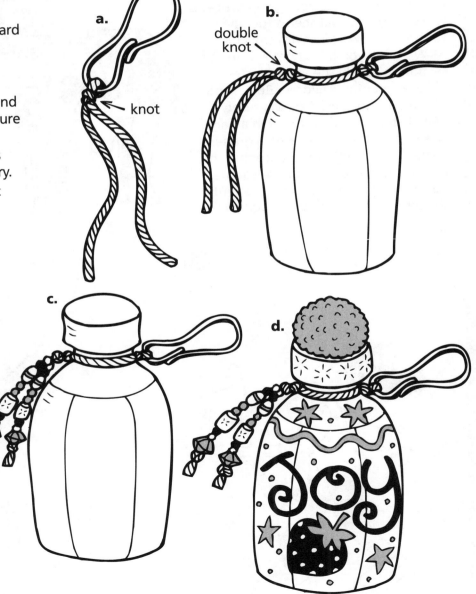

a. knot

b. double knot

c.

d. joy

Seed Packet Wall Hanging

(20-25 MINUTES)

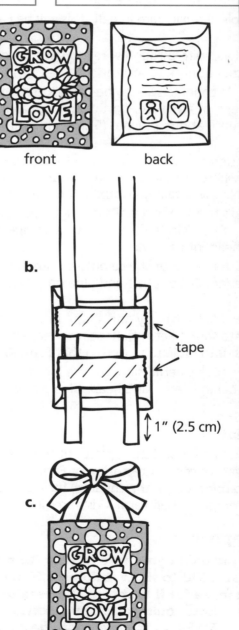

Materials
- ❖ Seed Packet Patterns (pp. 82-84)
- ❖ ½-inch (1.3-cm) grosgrain ribbon

Standard Supplies
- ❖ white card stock or copier paper
- ❖ scissors
- ❖ measuring stick
- ❖ crayons, colored pencils or fine-tip markers
- ❖ glue sticks
- ❖ masking tape

Preparation
Photocopy onto card stock or paper s̶ sets of Seed Packet Patterns, so there is a̶ least one packet pattern for each child. Cut two 18-inch (45.5-cm) lengths of ribbon for each child.

Instruct each child in the following procedures:

- Choose a Seed Packet Pattern. Color, cut out, fold and glue pattern to make a seed packet (see pattern page sketch and sketch a). (Note: Back side of packet will not be visible on finished craft.)
- Lay seed packet facedown on table. Tape two lengths of ribbon to seed packet as shown in sketch b.
- Turn seed packet right side up.
- Tie long ends of ribbon together in a bow above seed packet to make a hanger (sketch c).
- Trim ends of ribbon if necessary. Dab a small amount of glue on ends to keep them from fraying.

Enrichment Idea
Children make several or all five seed packets and hang from longer ribbons (see Enrichment Idea sketch). Allow an additional 5 inches (12.5 cm) of ribbon for each additional seed packet.

The Farm Report
What are some things that farmers grow from seeds? These seed packets show good things that can grow in our lives if we ask God to help us. What are they? (Love, joy, peace, patience and kindness.) **Your wall hangings can remind you to keep growing—and showing—the fruit of the Spirit. How is it possible for us to have peace?** (We can trust that God cares for us.) **What can you do to show love? Patience? Kindness? What has God done that gives you joy?**

a.

front   back

b.

tape

1" (2.5 cm)

c.

Enrichment Idea

Farm Kid (20-25 MINUTES)

Materials
- ❖ Hair Patterns
- ❖ Clothing Patterns
- ❖ chenille wires in various colors
- ❖ modeling clay

Standard Supplies
- ❖ white card stock
- ❖ scissors
- ❖ construction paper
- ❖ fine-tip colored markers
- ❖ glue

Preparation
Photocopy Hair and Clothing Patterns onto card stock and cut out several of each pattern.

Instruct each child in the following procedures:

- Cut one chenille wire in half. Form one half into a loop and twist the ends together (sketch a). This will be Farm Kid's head and neck.
- Fold another whole chenille wire in half. This will be Farm Kid's body and legs.
- Hook bend of folded wire through wire loop at the neck (sketch b). Twist wires together at neck to secure.
- Use another whole chenille wire to be Farm Kid's arms. About 2 inches (5 cm) from one end of arm wire, start wrapping around Farm Kid's body (sketch c). Wrap until about 2 inches (5 cm) remain for the second arm (sketch c).
- Trace clothing patterns of your choice onto folded construction paper, placing on folds where indicated, or make your own clothing design. Cut out clothing. Draw details on clothing if desired.
- Squeeze Farm Kid's head so that it fits through neck opening of clothing; place clothing on Farm Kid (sketch d). Glue side openings of clothing closed. Reshape head into an oval.
- Trace one hair pattern of your choice onto construction paper, or make your own hair design. Cut out hair and glue onto Farm Kid's head (sketch e).
- Take a grape-sized lump of clay and shape into a shoe. Insert one of Farm Kid's legs into shoe (sketch f). Repeat to make a second shoe. Press bottoms of shoes onto table to flatten so that Farm Kid stands upright.
- At home, with an adult's permission, cut the face from a photograph of yourself to fit behind Farm Kid's head. Glue picture to chenille wire (sketch g).

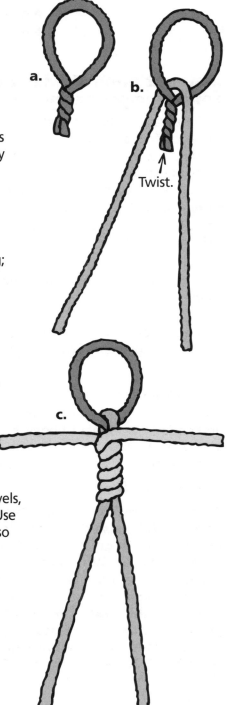

a.

b.

Twist.

c.

Enrichment Ideas

Kids use construction paper and short pieces of chenille wire to make shovels, rakes, carrots, flowers or other accessories for Farm Kids to hold or wear. Use a digital camera to photograph the children; have a helper print photos so that children can complete their Farm Kids' faces in class.

The Farm Report

At home, glue a picture of your face to your Farm Kid's head. You can bend your Farm Kid to show it doing different things. What object could you make for it that could be used to do something kind for someone? How could you show kindness with (a book)? First Thessalonians 5:15 says, *Always try to be kind to each other and to everyone else.*

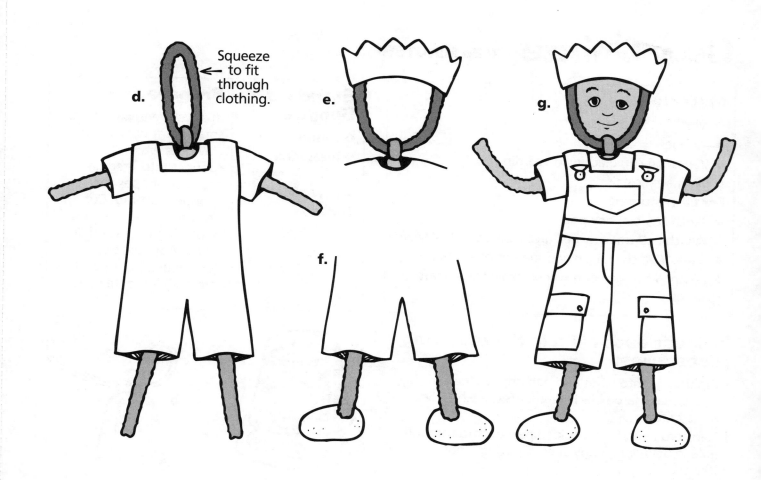

d. Squeeze to fit through clothing.

e.

f.

g.

Clothing Patterns

fold   fold

fold   fold

fold

Hair Patterns

Cow Chime (20-25 MINUTES)

Materials
- white flat spray paint
- sponges
- ¼-inch (.6-cm) black nylon cording
- black acrylic paint

For each student—
- 3-inch (7.5-cm) clay pot
- ¾-inch (1.9-cm) cow bell (available at craft stores)
- three 1/2-inch (1.3-cm) wooden or plastic beads
- 2-inch (5-cm) wooden wheel (available at craft stores)

Standard Supplies
- scissors
- measuring stick
- newspaper
- shallow containers

Preparation
In a well-ventilated area, spray-paint outsides of clay pots white. Cut sponges into irregular rounded shapes for sponge painting. Cut one 2-foot (.6-m) length of cording for each child. Cover work area with newspaper. Pour paint into shallow containers.

Instruct each child in the following procedures:

- Dip sponge into paint and dab onto outside of clay pot to make large black cow spots (sketch a). Set aside to dry.
- Fold cord in half. Tuck folded part of cord through hole in bell; bring ends of cord through loop (sketch b).
- Holding cord strands together, tie a knot about 2 inches (5 cm) above the bell. Thread strands through a bead and then through wooden wheel (sketch c).
- Holding strands together, tie a knot about 3 inches (7.5 cm) above wheel. Thread strands through a second bead and then through hole in bottom of clay pot (sketch d).
- Make sure wheel strikes inside of clay pot somewhere near the bottom edge. If necessary, adjust knot so that it does.
- Thread strands through a third bead directly above clay pot (sketch e).
- Knot cord ends together to make a hanger (sketch e).

Simplification Idea
Do not spray-paint clay pots. Have children paint white splotches on pot for a brown and white cow pattern.

The Farm Report
How could hanging a bell around a cow's neck keep it from getting lost? If you can't SEE the cow, you can HEAR the bell! If you lost a cow, and then you heard its bell ring, how might you feel? (Happy. Joyful.) **The Bible says that's how God feels when we are "lost"—when we do wrong things—but then we ask Him to forgive us. When you hear your Cow Chime ring, it can remind you of God's joy.**

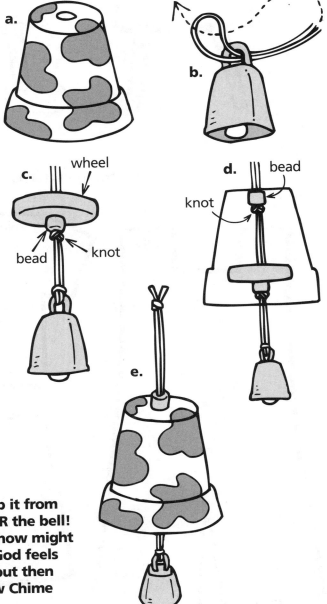

a.

b.

c. wheel
bead   knot

d. bead
knot

e.

Growing Love Topiary (20-25 MINUTES)

Materials
- ❖ several pairs of pliers
- ❖ drill with ¼-inch (.6-cm) drill bit
- ❖ acrylic paints in various colors
- ❖ potting soil
- ❖ several small cups for scooping soil

For each child—
- ❖ lightweight rubber-coated wire coat hanger
- ❖ empty 20-oz. or larger vegetable or coffee can
- ❖ small ivy plant

Standard Supplies
- ❖ newspaper
- ❖ shallow containers
- ❖ paintbrushes
- ❖ water

Preparation
Use pliers to straighten coat hangers as much as possible. (Note: It is not necessary to fully straighten spiral sections of hanger.) Remove any labels from cans. Drill three drainage holes in bottom of each can (sketch a). Cover work area with newspaper. Pour paints into shallow containers.

Instruct each child in the following procedures:

- Paint outside of can to decorate. Set aside to dry.
- Fold coat hanger in half. Starting at the top, bend wire to make the outline of a cross or a heart, leaving extra wire at the bottom to anchor in soil (sketch b). If necessary, use pliers or edge of table to help bend wire.
- Scoop several inches of soil into can. Place ivy plant in can and fill pot with more soil.
- Insert ends of wire deep into soil to secure (sketch c).
- Gently wrap ivy around wire (sketch d).
- Pour a small amount of water into can.
- Keep plant in a bright spot, away from direct sunlight. Water whenever soil feels dry. As ivy grows it will continue to climb around wire frame.

Simplification Idea
Bend wire frames ahead of time.

The Farm Report
A plant that is made to grow in a decorative shape is called a topiary. What does the shape of your topiary remind you of? (Jesus. God's love.) **What did Jesus do that showed God's love? Jesus said,** *My command is this: Love each other as I have loved you* **(John 15:12). What can WE do to follow Jesus' example of loving others?** (Forgive others. Help someone who is sick or in need. Pray for people. Tell people about God's love.)

a. holes

b.

c.

d.

Joyful Message Board (20-25 MINUTES)

Materials
❖ Styrofoam insulation board (available at hardware stores)
❖ cork sheeting (available at hardware, office supply or art supply stores)
❖ white and pink Fun Foam
❖ blue, green and white acrylic paints

For each child—
❖ three T-pins (available at craft and office supply stores)
❖ three 1½-inch (4-cm) white pom-poms
❖ six medium-sized wiggle eyes

Standard Supplies
❖ craft knife
❖ ruler
❖ scissors
❖ newspaper
❖ shallow containers
❖ craft glue
❖ paintbrushes

Preparation
Use craft knife to cut one 10x12-inch (25.5x30.5-cm) insulation-board rectangle for each child. Use scissors to cut one 10x12-inch (25.5x30.5-cm) cork-sheeting rectangle for each child. Cut four ½x12-inch (1.3x30.5-cm) white Fun Foam strips for each child. Cut one 2-inch (5-cm) square of pink Fun Foam for each child. Cover work area with newspaper. Pour paints into shallow containers.

Instruct each child in the following procedures:
• Glue cork sheet to insulation board.
• Paint a blue sky and white clouds on top quarter of corkboard; paint a green hillside on rest of board (sketch a). Set aside to dry.
• Insert a T-pin as far as it will go through the center of each pom-pom (sketch b).
• Glue two wiggle eyes on each pom-pom just above T-pin (sketch b).
• For each sheep, cut two ears and a nose from pink Fun Foam. Glue ears and noses onto sheep (sketch b). Set aside to dry.
• Cut two white foam strips into quarters to make fence pickets (sketch c).
• Place pickets along bottom of corkboard to make an evenly spaced fence. Glue the outermost right and left pickets to the board. Glue only the bottom edge of all other pickets to the board (sketch d). (The finished fence will be a pocket.)
• Place two dots of glue on each picket and glue the two uncut foam strips across pickets (sketch e).
• When message board is completely dry, insert sheep pins into cork. At home, use sheep pins to tack notes to board, or tuck them behind picket fence.

Simplification Idea
Omit foam fences. Children paint fences on message boards.

Enrichment Ideas
Children paint flowers, trees and a farm on message boards. They make larger message boards and make additional sheep pins.

The Farm Report
Jesus told a story about a shepherd who lost one sheep. Because the shepherd loved the sheep, he searched and searched until he found it. Then he carefully placed it on his shoulders and carried it back to the flock. He was so happy that he called all his friends to celebrate. How do you think God is like that shepherd? Jesus said that God always loves us. When anyone becomes a member of His family, He is so joyful that He celebrates. Your Joyful Message Board can remind you of how much God loves each one of us.

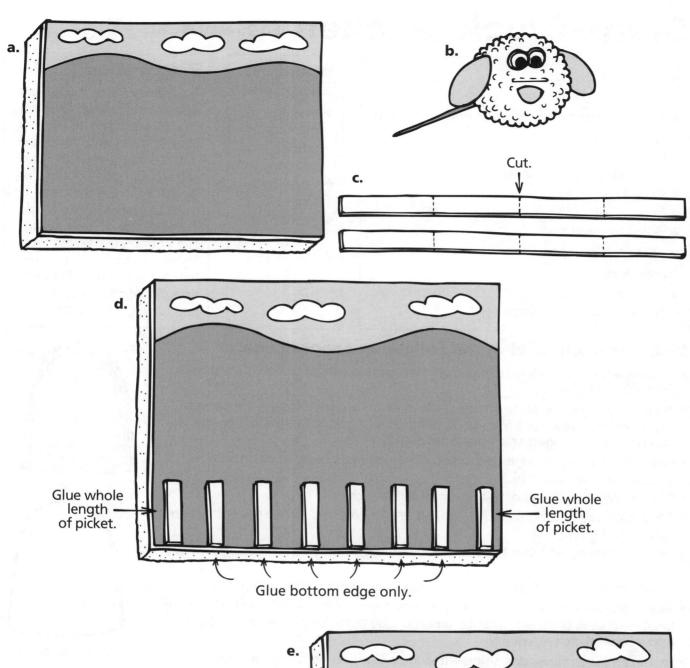

a.

b.

c.

Cut.

d.

Glue whole length of picket. → Glue whole length of picket. ←

Glue bottom edge only.

e.

Cluck-Cluck Chicken (20-25 MINUTES)

Materials
- ❖ Cluck-Cluck Chicken Patterns
- ❖ variety of fabrics in solid colors and small prints
- ❖ cotton string
- ❖ nail
- ❖ 2-inch (5-cm) Styrofoam balls
- ❖ sharp knife
- ❖ iron
- ❖ yellow and red felt
- ❖ paper or old towels

For each child—
- ❖ 10-oz. plastic cup
- ❖ two medium-sized wiggle eyes

Standard Supplies
- ❖ fine-tip markers
- ❖ fabric scissors
- ❖ white card stock
- ❖ measuring stick
- ❖ craft glue

Preparation
Trace Body Pattern onto fabric and cut out two for each child. Trace Comb, Wattle and Beak Patterns onto card stock and cut out several of each pattern. Cut one 2-foot (.6-m) length of string for each child. Use nail to poke a hole in the center of each plastic cup bottom. Use knife to cut Styrofoam balls in half, one half for each child. Plug in iron out of children's reach and turn to a low setting.

Instruct each child in the following procedures:

- Squeeze a continuous line of glue along top and side edges of body fabric piece, print side up (sketch a).
- Place matching fabric piece on top of glued piece, print side down. Press edges together. Place paper or towels underneath and on top of fabric and iron the two fabric pieces together, so glue dries quickly.
- Poke end of string through hole in cup. Tie string in a double knot on outside of cup to secure (sketch b).
- Glue Styrofoam ball half onto bottom of cup (sketch b).
- Trace Comb and Wattle Patterns onto red felt and cut out. Trace Beak Pattern onto yellow felt and cut out.
- Carefully turn glued fabric pieces inside out and slide over cup and Styrofoam ball (sketch c).
- Glue bottom edge of fabric to inside of cup, making sure string is kept free (sketch d).
- Glue comb piece on top of chicken head along seam. Glue wiggle eyes on sides of head. Fold beak piece along center line and glue onto head. Glue wattle piece under beak (sketch e). Let dry.
- To make chicken cluck: Wet string with water. Grasp string firmly between fingers and slide fingers down string in a quick motion (sketch f). Experiment with different techniques and sounds!

Simplification Ideas
Glue or sew chicken body fabric pieces together ahead of time. Or have children place small thin socks over cups and Styrofoam balls.

The Farm Report
What do you think is the difference between a white egg and a brown egg? God made over 150 different kinds of chickens that can be raised on a farm. Chickens with white feathers lay white eggs, and red or brown chickens usually lay brown eggs. Some chickens lay pink, green or blue eggs! But all colors of eggs are the same inside. God also made people who look different from each other. People sometimes think it's okay to treat others differently depending on how they look. But the Bible tells us to be kind to ALL our neighbors. And who do you think Jesus said our neighbors are? (Everyone.)

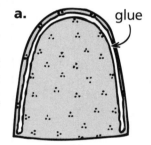

a.

glue

print side up

print side down

b.

glue

double knot

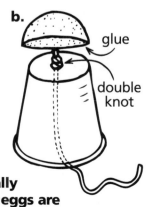

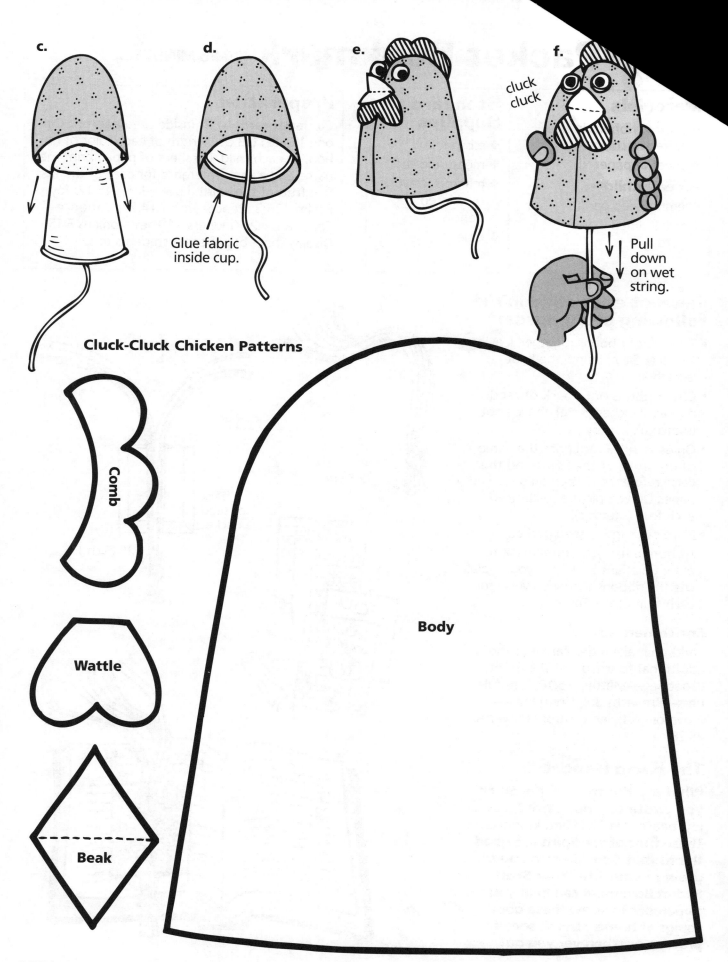

c.

d. Glue fabric inside cup.

e.

f. cluck cluck

Pull down on wet string.

Cluck-Cluck Chicken Patterns

Comb

Wattle

Beak

Body

cket Bookmark (20-25 MINUTES)

Standard Supplies
- ❖ scissors
- ❖ measuring stick
- ❖ markers, crayons or colored pencils
- ❖ glue

Preparation
Cut index cards to fit inside seed packets. Cut one 15-inch (38-cm) length of each color of ribbon for each child. On sheet of paper, print the name and a verse reference for each of the first five fruit of the Spirit: Love—John 15:12; Joy—Psalm 126:3; Peace—John 14:27; Patience—Ephesians 4:2; Kindness—1 Thessalonians 5:15. Display sheet of paper for students to see.

Instruct each child in the following procedures:

- Tie ends of ribbons together, leaving 1 inch (2.5 cm) below the knot (sketch a).
- Glue ribbons onto back of seed packet, 2 inches (5 cm) above knot (sketch b). Let dry.
- On each index card print the name of one fruit of the Spirit and the verse reference written on displayed paper. Draw a picture to illustrate each fruit (sketch c).
- Place cards inside seed packet.
- At home, use your bookmark to mark Galatians 5:22-23 in your Bible. Use the ribbons to mark a verse for each fruit of the Spirit.

Enrichment Idea
Children make index cards for the additional four fruit of the Spirit. (Goodness—Matthew 5:16; Faithfulness—Proverbs 3:3; Gentleness—Proverbs 15:1; Self-control—Proverbs 25:28.)

The Farm Report

What are the fruit of the Spirit you wrote on your cards? (Love, joy, peace, patience and kindness.) **These fruit of the Spirit are good things that God can help you to grow in your life. Your Seed Packet Bookmark can help you remember to show these good things at home, school, soccer practice or wherever you go!**

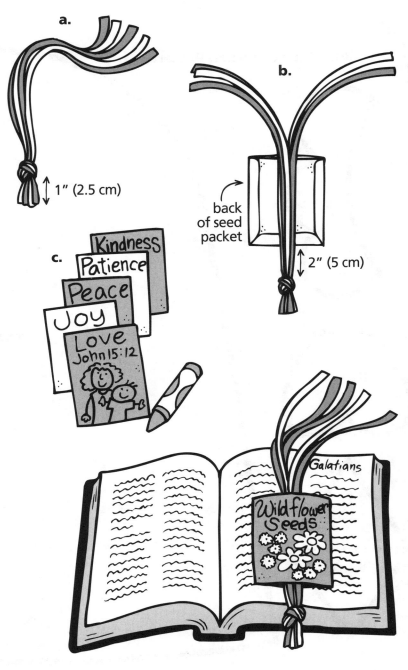

a.

1" (2.5 cm)

b.

back of seed packet

2" (5 cm)

c. Kindness Patience Peace Joy Love John 15:12

Galatians

Wildflower Seeds

60

Clothespin Cow (25-30 MINUTES)

Materials

- ❖ small saw
- ❖ heavy-duty scissors
- ❖ white flat spray paint
- ❖ wooden tongue depressors
- ❖ pink acrylic paint
- ❖ several low-temperature glue guns
- ❖ black yarn
- ❖ black permanent fine-tip markers

For each child—

- ❖ five large flat wooden clothespins (non-spring type)
- ❖ two small wiggle eyes

Standard Supplies

- ❖ newspaper
- ❖ shallow containers
- ❖ scissors
- ❖ paintbrushes

Preparation

Saw one set of clothespins for each child as shown in sketch a. Cut off ends of tongue depressors and cut ends in half to make two cow's ears for each child (sketch b). Spray-paint clothespin and tongue depressor pieces white. Cover work area with newspaper. Pour paint into shallow containers. Plug in glue guns. (Note: Ensure that there is adequate adult supervision for each glue gun.)

Instruct each child in the following procedures:

- Paint udder piece pink (sketch c). Let dry.
- Glue ears and wiggle eyes onto cow's head (sketch d).
- Cut three short pieces of yarn and unravel them. Glue yarn pieces onto top of cow's head (sketch d).
- Glue middle body pieces together. Glue the two uncut clothespins onto either side of body. Glue udder piece underneath body (sketch e).
- Glue head onto one end of cow, at an angle so that head is cocked (sketch f).
- Cut a short piece of yarn for the cow's tail. Tie a knot near one end. Unravel small section of yarn below knot. Glue tail onto rear of cow's body.
- Use marker to draw spots on cow. Draw nostrils on cow's face (sketch f).

Simplification Idea

Eliminate spray painting cow pieces white and leave wood its natural color.

The Farm Report

When have you seen a herd of cows grazing on a green hill? How would you describe them? Peaceful? Worried? The Bible says God takes care of animals and birds, and He takes care of us, too. When we're worried, we can remember that God takes care of us. We can have peace.

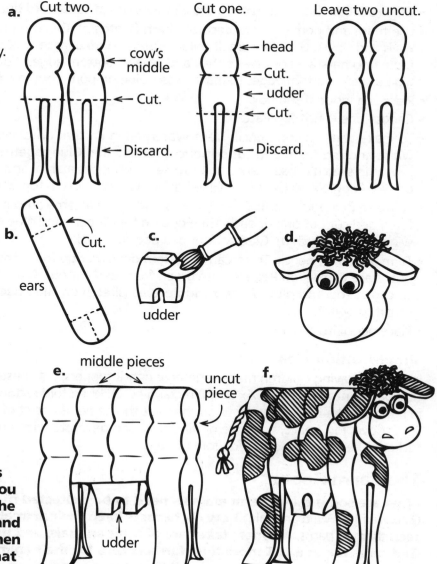

a. Cut two. Cut one. Leave two uncut.
cow's middle — head — Cut. — udder — Cut. — Discard.

b. Cut. ears

c. udder

d.

e. middle pieces uncut piece udder

f.

Pencil Barn (20-25 MINUTES)

Materials
- ❖ Barn Pattern
- ❖ Pencil Top Patterns
- ❖ Fun Foam in red, green, white, orange and yellow
- ❖ black permanent fine-tip markers
- ❖ small pom-poms in various flower colors
- ❖ small wiggle eyes

For each student—
- ❖ square tissue box
- ❖ empty large vegetable or soup can
- ❖ unsharpened pencil

Standard Supplies
- ❖ white card stock
- ❖ scissors
- ❖ craft glue

Preparation
Trace Barn Pattern onto red Fun Foam, adjusting if necessary to fit tissue boxes; for each child, cut out two complete barn shapes and two rectangles (follow three solid lines and the dashed line). Trace Pencil Top Patterns onto card stock to make several copies of each pattern and cut out.

Instruct each child in the following procedures:

- Glue red foam barn cutouts around all four sides of cardboard box to make a barn (sketch a).
- Use foam and pom-poms to decorate barn (sketch b). Glue on narrow strips of white foam to outline walls and doors. Glue four small yellow squares onto a large white square to make a window. Cut yellow foam into haystacks or bales of hay and glue to bottom edges. Cut strips of green foam into fringe and glue around bottom edges to make grass. Glue on pom-poms for flowers.
- Place can inside tissue box.
- Choose one Pencil Top Pattern.
- To make watermelon pencil: Trace Watermelon Pattern onto green, white and red foam and cut out one of each color. Glue together as shown in sketch c. Use marker to draw seeds on watermelon, and glue on two wiggle eyes (sketch c). Glue back of watermelon to top of pencil.
- To make pea pod pencil: Trace Pea Pod and Peas Patterns onto green foam and cut out one of each. Glue pod on top of peas and glue on six wiggle eyes (sketch d). Glue back of pea pod to pencil.
- To make carrot pencil: Trace Carrot Pattern onto orange foam and cut out. Trace Carrot Top Pattern onto green foam and cut out. Glue carrot to carrot top and glue on two wiggle eyes (sketch e). Glue back of carrot to pencil.
- Place pencil inside can.

a.

Simplification Idea
Instead of having children make vegetable pencil toppers, cut construction paper into 1x4-inch (2.5x10-cm) rectangles. Children fold rectangles in half to make flags. They write on the flags the name of a fruit of the Spirit (love, joy, peace, patience or kindness) and decorate with small stickers. They glue pencils inside fold of flags.

b.

The Farm Report
What are some things farm animals need to be protected from? (Bad weather. Wild animals.) **How do farmers keep their animals safe?** (They keep them in barns.) **Farmers take care of their animals, and they protect them. God cares for us a LOT more than farmers care for their animals. What are some ways God cares for us? When was a time God protected you or someone you know?**

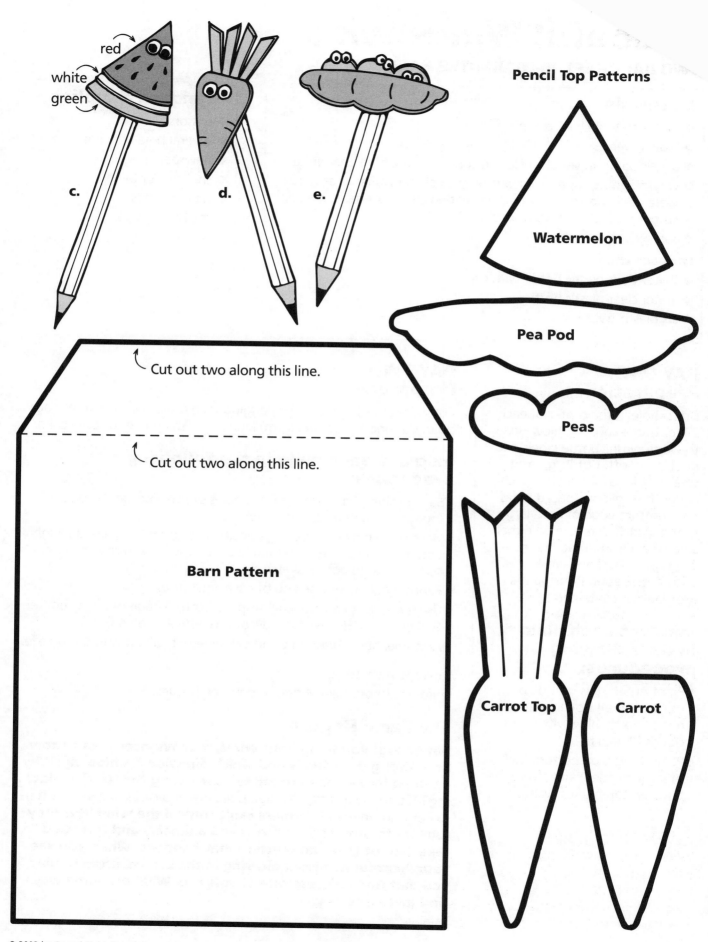

red

white

green

c.

d.

e.

Pencil Top Patterns

Watermelon

Pea Pod

Peas

Cut out two along this line.

Cut out two along this line.

Barn Pattern

Carrot Top

Carrot

...ul Windsock

...rials

- ...ill with ¼-inch (.6-cm) bit
- blow-dryer
- acrylic paints in various colors including green, blue and white
- vinyl flagging tape in various bright colors (available at hardware or garden stores) or vinyl sheeting cut into 1-inch (2.5-cm) strips (available at hardware stores)
- fishing line

For each child—
- 2-liter clear plastic bottle with cap
- 1-liter clear plastic bottle
- six plastic twist ties

Standard Supplies
- scissors
- several hole punches
- newspaper
- shallow containers
- paintbrushes
- measuring stick

DAY ONE
Preparation

Drill a hole in the center of each 2-liter bottle cap. Use blow-dryer to warm plastic bottle labels and peel them off. Cut large and small bottles as shown in sketch a. Punch six evenly spaced holes near bottom edge of each large bottle. Punch one hole on either side of each small bottle, near the top edge. Cover work area with newspaper. Pour paints into shallow containers.

Instruct each child in the following procedures:

- Paint green hills on bottom third of small bottle. Paint rest of bottle blue with white clouds (sketch b).
- Paint flowers on bottom half of large bottle. Paint flying birds on top half of bottle (sketch c).

DAY TWO
Preparation

Cut six 3-foot (.9-m) strips of flagging tape or vinyl sheeting for each child. Cut one 18-inch (45.5-cm) length of fishing line for each child.

Instruct each child in the following procedures:

- String fishing line through both holes of small bottle. Tie ends together in a double knot (sketch d).
- Place small bottle inside large bottle, pushing fishing line through bottle opening. Thread fishing line through hole in cap and screw cap onto large bottle (sketch e).
- Punch a hole near one end of each vinyl strip.
- Use twist ties to attach vinyl strips to bottom edge of larger bottle. Curl ends of twist ties for a decorative effect (sketch f).
- At home, hang Peaceful Windsock where it will blow in the breeze.

Enrichment Idea
Children choose own design to paint on bottles.

The Farm Report
Where will you hang your windsock? Windsocks can show how strong the wind is and which direction it's blowing. Why would a farmer need to know how strong the wind is blowing? (Strong winds can damage buildings and crops, blow away topsoil or hurt animals.) **Farmers can't control the wind. But they CAN try to protect their farms and animals—and trust God to take care of them no matter what happens. When you see your Peaceful Windsock blowing in the breeze, it can remind you that God will take care of you, too. What are some ways God takes care of us?**

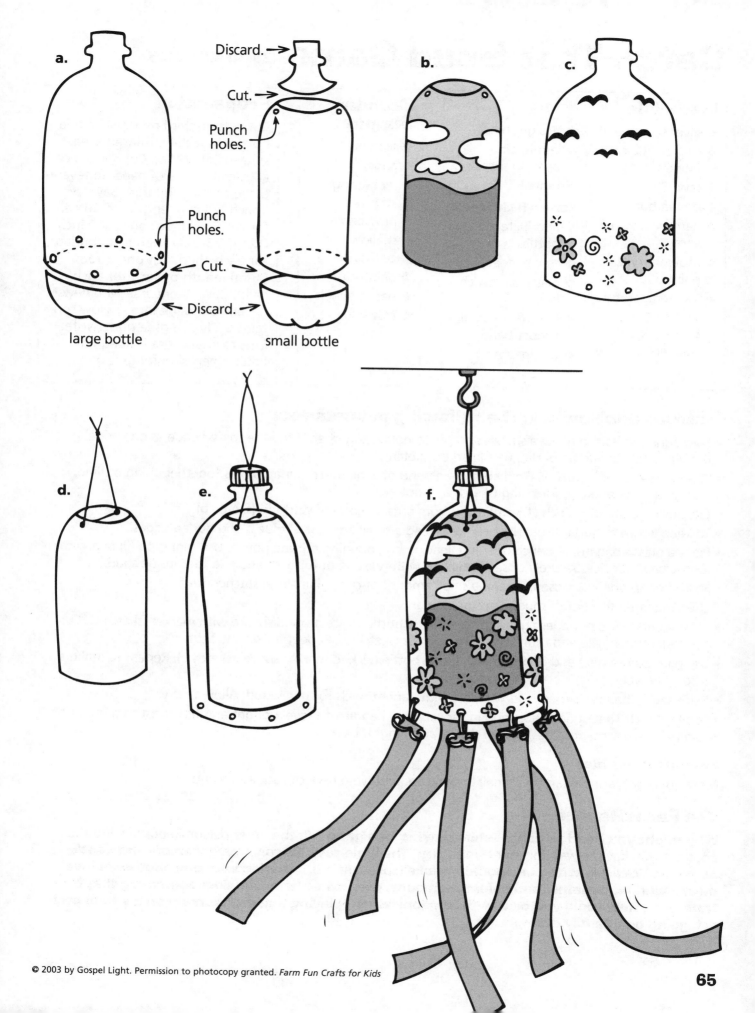

Catch-That-Spud Game (25-30 MINUTES)

Materials
- silver spray paint
- 7/8-inch (2.2-cm) dowels
- saw
- brown burlap
- narrow brown yarn
- brown acrylic paint
- low-temperature glue gun
- permanent markers
- straight pins
- lentils, pinto beans or rice
- funnel

For each child—
- two 2-liter soda bottles
- crewel needle
- plastic sandwich bag
- twist tie or small rubber band
- sandpaper

Standard Supplies
- scissors
- paper
- measuring stick
- newspaper
- shallow containers
- paintbrushes
- paper towels
- craft glue

Preparation
Cut bottom third off of each soda bottle. In well-ventilated area, spray-paint bottles. Cut one 5-inch (12.5-cm) square of paper for every three or four children. Saw two 9-inch (23-cm) lengths of dowel for each child. Cut one 5x10-inch (12.5x25.5-cm) rectangle of burlap for each child. Cut one 2-foot (.6-m) length of yarn for each child. Cover work area with newspaper. Pour paint into shallow containers. Plug in glue gun. (Note: Ensure that there is adequate adult supervision for glue gun.)

Instruct each child in the following procedures:
- Fold burlap in half to make a square and pin to hold it together. Using the folded edge as one edge, draw a potato shape on burlap with marker (sketch a).
- Thread needle with yarn. Make a knot in one end of yarn. Stitch burlap pieces together along outline, leaving a small opening for filling (sketch a). Knot end.
- Cut out spud about ½ inch (1.3 cm) away from outside edge of stitching (sketch b).
- To keep edges of burlap from unraveling, spread a small amount of glue along burlap edges.
- Place a plastic bag inside pouch opening, leaving bag opening outside pouch. Use funnel to fill bag with lentils, beans or rice. Securely close plastic bag with twist tie or rubber band and tuck inside spud.
- Stitch burlap opening closed. Spread a small amount of craft glue along stitched seam.
- Use sandpaper to smooth rough ends on dowels.
- Hold square piece of paper against edge of soda bottle. Trace around square with marker (sketch c). Cut out square on bottle and round off sharp corners (sketch d). Repeat for second bottle.
- Use glue gun to glue end of one dowel inside bottle neck to make a shovel (sketch e). Repeat to make a second shovel.
- Paint shovel handles brown and wipe off with paper towels to stain wood. Allow to dry.
- To play Catch-That-Spud: Place spud in shovel. Hold handle of shovel upright and flick wrist to fling spud to a partner. Partner catches spud in shovel and flings it back.

Simplification Idea
Make spud by placing beans in a small brown sock and tying neck of sock into a knot.

The Farm Report
Why might you need patience while playing this game? (If the other person keeps missing the potato. If you have to wait for your turn to play.) **The Bible says, *Be completely humble and gentle; be patient, bearing with one another in love* (Ephesians 4:2). "Bearing with one another in love" means working together and helping someone, even when he or she does something that frustrates you. How could you bear with someone when (playing a game, working on a school project, going on a family outing)?**

a. fold — Leave unsewn for opening. — yarn

b.

c.

d. Cut.

e.

Scarecrow Plant Stake

(ONE OR TWO-DAY CRAFT/15-20 MINUTES EACH DAY)

Materials
- raffia
- fabric in a variety of small prints
- burlap
- felt
- yarn
- black permanent fine-tip markers

For each child—
- two small wiggle eyes
- bamboo skewer

Standard Supplies
- scissors
- rulers
- craft glue

DAY ONE
Preparation

Cut raffia into 12-inch (30.5-cm) lengths to make about a ¾-inch (1.9-cm)-thick bundle for each child.

Instruct each child in the following procedures:

- Set aside seven strands of raffia from your bundle to use as ties.
- Tie one strand of raffia around center of bundle and trim ends of tie (sketch a).
- Bend raffia bundle in half with tied part at top. Wrap a strand of raffia around doubled bundle and knot securely to make scarecrow head (sketch b).
- Separate a few strands from each side of scarecrow for arms. Tie a strand of raffia around center of each bundle. Trim ends of raffia below each knot to make hands (sketch b).
- Tie a strand of raffia around remaining raffia bundle to form waist (sketch c).
- Divide raffia below scarecrow's waist into two even sections for legs. Tie a strand of raffia near the end of each section to make feet (sketch c).

DAY TWO
Preparation

Cut one 4-inch (10-cm) fabric square for each child. Cut one 2-inch (5-cm) circle of burlap for each child. Cut one ½x4-inch (1.3x10-cm) felt strip for each child. Cut one 6-inch (15-cm) length of yarn for each child.

Instruct each child in the following procedures:

- Fold fabric square into quarters. Cut out a quarter circle from folded corner of fabric to make a neck hole. Cut out a 1¼-inch (3-cm) square from unfolded corner of fabric to make sleeves (sketch d).
- Unfold fabric and cut a small slit on one side of neck hole (sketch e).
- Place shirt over scarecrow's head. Glue shirt together under arms and along sides. Tie yarn piece securely around the waist and trim ends (sketch f).
- Glue felt piece around neck and overlap in front to make a collar (sketch f).
- Cut a slit to the center of burlap circle (sketch g). Overlap and glue in place to form a slightly cone-shaped hat (sketch h). Glue hat onto head.
- Glue wiggle eyes onto scarecrow face. Use marker to draw mouth and nose.
- Place a small amount of glue on dull end of skewer and insert into back of scarecrow, underneath shirt (sketch h).
- At home, stick skewer in the soil of a potted plant to display your scarecrow.

Enrichment Idea
Older children design their own scarecrow clothes using fabric, burlap and felt.

The Farm Report
What are scarecrows used for? They scare crows! Animals and birds love to eat the plants in a garden. When they see a scarecrow, they think it's a real person and they stay away from the garden. Everyone is scared sometimes. What are some things that people today are scared of? (Going to a new school. Speaking to a large group of people.) **Praying to God when we're afraid and worried can help us have peace.**

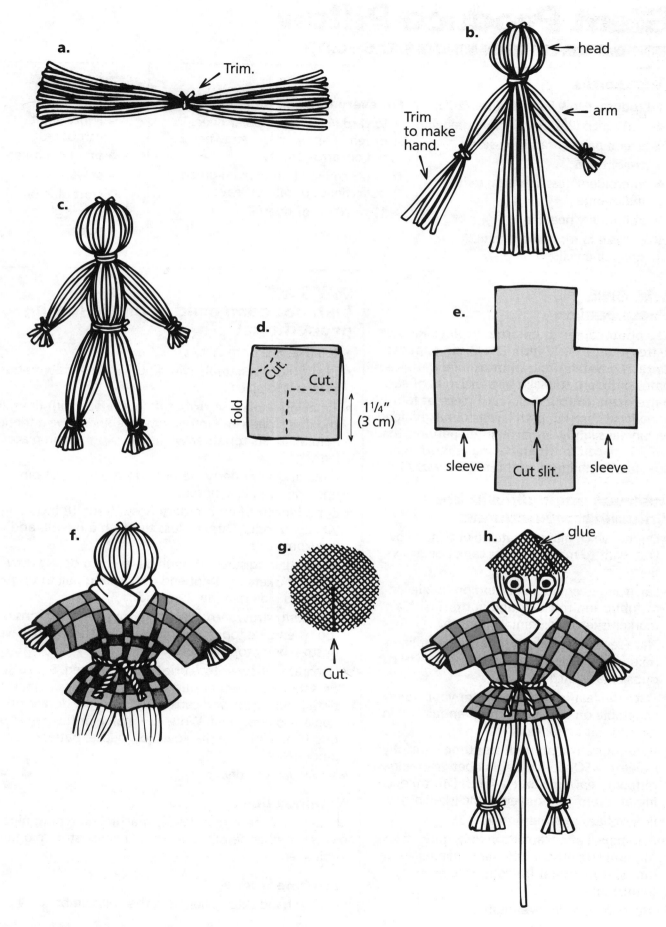

a. Trim.

b. head — arm — Trim to make hand.

c.

d. fold — Cut. — Cut. — 1¼″ (3 cm)

e. sleeve — Cut slit. — sleeve

f.

g. Cut.

h. glue

Giant Produce Pillow

(TWO-DAY CRAFT/25-30 MINUTES EACH DAY)

Materials
- ❖ Produce Pillow Patterns (pp. 72-75)
- ❖ 11x17-inch (28x43-cm) copier paper
- ❖ several pairs of fabric scissors
- ❖ straight pins
- ❖ embroidery floss in green, red and orange
- ❖ embroidery needles
- ❖ squeeze fabric paint in pink, green and yellow

For every three to four children—
- ❖ ½ yard (45.5 cm) of polar fleece or felt in apple green, strawberry red or carrot orange
- ❖ ¼ (23 cm) yard of medium green polar fleece or felt for leaves
- ❖ 15 to 20 oz. of fiberfill

Standard Supplies
- ❖ lightweight cardboard
- ❖ fine-tip markers
- ❖ scissors
- ❖ craft glue or fabric glue
- ❖ rulers

DAY ONE
Preparation
Use photocopier to enlarge Produce Pillow Patterns onto 11x17-inch (28x43-cm) paper as large as possible. Trace photocopied patterns onto cardboard to make several copies of each pattern and cut out. Fold each piece of fabric in half; cut through both layers to make folded rectangles slightly larger than the patterns that will be placed on them (to make more manageable for children and to reduce waste).

Instruct each child in the following procedures:
- Decide which giant vegetable or fruit pillow you want to make—apple, carrot or strawberry.
- Lay fruit or vegetable pattern on two layers of fabric and trace around pattern with a marker (sketch a). Remove pattern.
- Place several pins along inside edge of line to hold fabric layers together. Use scissors to cut out shape (sketch b).
- Trace the leaf or top pattern for your fruit or vegetable on two layers of green fabric. Pin and cut out as above.
- Keeping fabric pinned together, carefully squeeze a SOLID line of glue between edges of fabric, leaving about a 4-inch (10-cm) opening at top of fruit or vegetable (sketch c).
- Press edges together firmly.
- For apple leaf or carrot top only, glue edges of fabric together in the same manner, leaving an opening at bottom of leaf or top (sketch d).
- Allow glue to dry overnight.

DAY TWO
Instruct each child in the following procedures:
- Remove pins from pillow.
- Stuff fruit or vegetable with fiberfill. Use a ruler to push it deep into pillow.
- If making apple or carrot, stuff leaf or top with fiberfill and insert open end into pillow opening. Have a friend hold all layers together while you pin them in place (sketch e).
- If making strawberry, do not add top yet. Just pin opening of pillow closed.
- Cut a length of embroidery floss about 18 inches (45.5 cm) long. Thread floss through a needle and knot one end.
- Sew a running stitch through all layers to close pillow opening (sketch f). Knot end of floss and pull through pillow to hide it inside. Trim ends.
- If making strawberry, glue together stem sections of top. Then glue top of strawberry pillow between leaves of strawberry top (sketch g).
- Decorate pillow with fabric paint if desired. Squeeze dots to make seeds on strawberry, draw lines to make details on carrot and carrot top, or draw details on apple and apple leaf. Write your name or the name of one fruit of the Spirit—love, joy, peace, patience or kindness.
- Allow paint to dry.

Simplification
Make this craft in one day by machine-stitching pillow pieces together before class time. Children stuff and finish as directed.

Enrichment Idea
Children hand-stitch pillow together with embroidery floss.

The Farm Report

What are some things farmers do to help their crops to grow? (Plow the soil. Fertilize the soil. Plant the seeds. Water the plants.) **Farmers work hard all year to help their crops produce good fruits and vegetables. But who really makes the plants grow?** (God.) **The Bible says that** *the fruit of the Spirit is love, joy, peace, patience, kindness, goodness, faithfulness, gentleness and self-control* (Galatians 5:22-23). **What are some things we can do to stay close to God?** (Pray. Read the Bible. Go to church. Learn from other Christians.) **All those things will help the fruit of the Spirit grow in our lives, but it's God who truly makes us grow. Your Produce Pillow can remind you to stay close to God, so He can help you produce the fruit of the Spirit.**

a. pattern

b. pin

c. Leave opening unglued. Glue

d. opening opening

e. insert

f.

g. glue Glue pillow between leaves.

Patience Joy Kindness

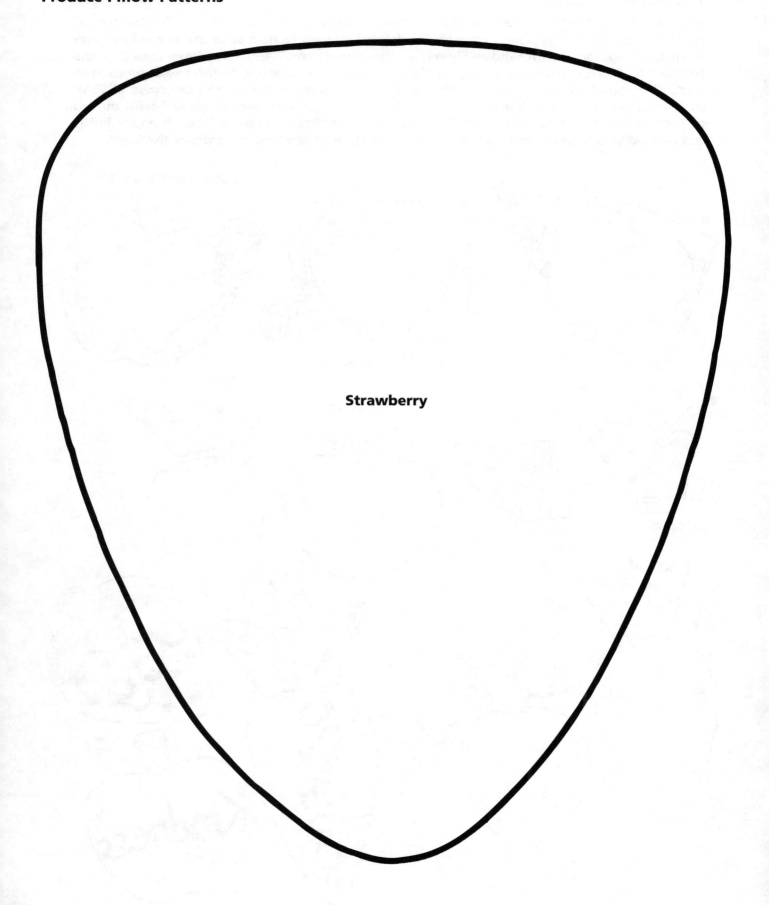

Strawberry

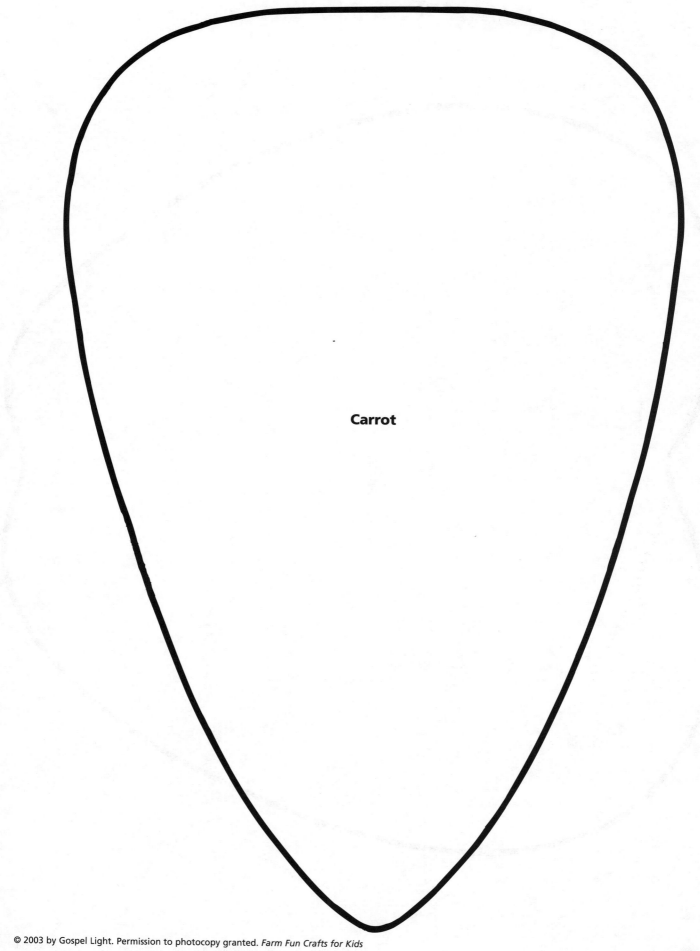

Carrot

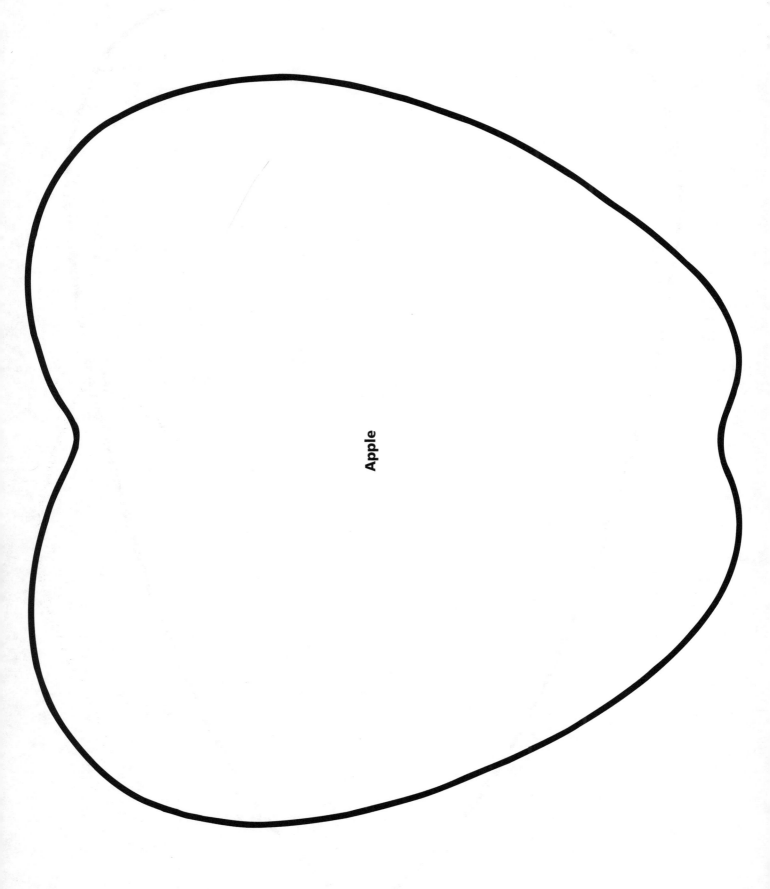

Apple

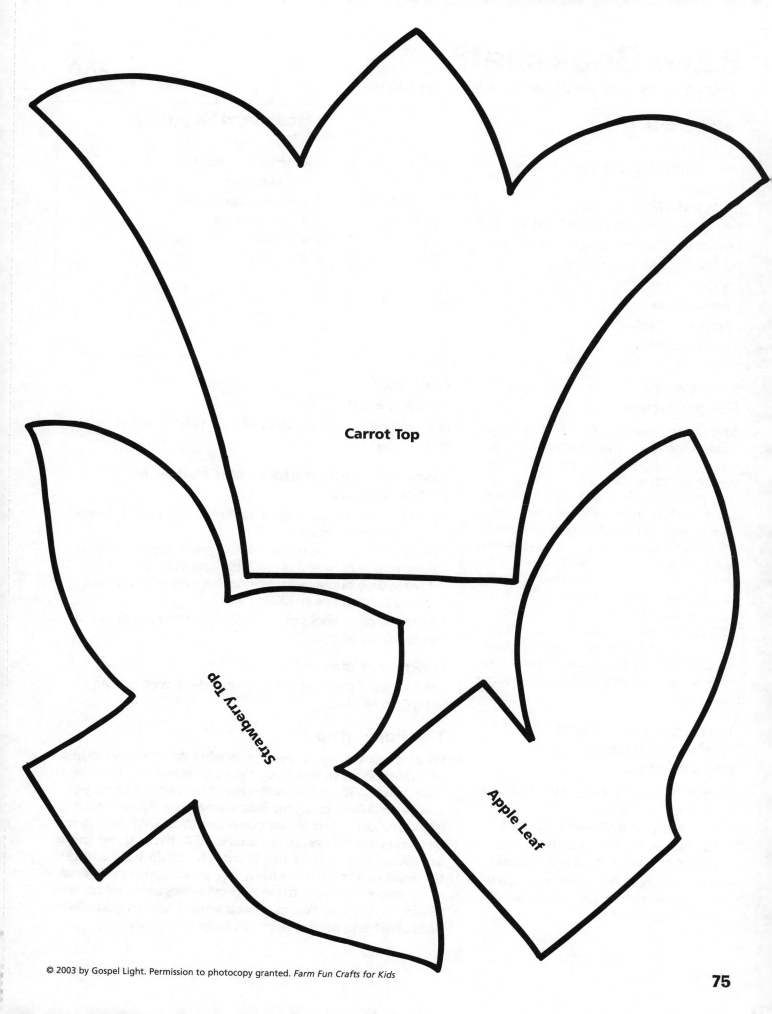

Carrot Top

Strawberry Top

Apple Leaf

Barn Bookshelf
(TWO-DAY CRAFT/20-25 MINUTES EACH DAY)

Materials
- ❖ Cow Pattern
- ❖ 1x6-inch (2.5x15-cm) pine boards
- ❖ saw
- ❖ ½-inch (1.3-cm) dowels
- ❖ drill with ½-inch (1.3-cm) and ⅝-inch (1.6-cm) drill bits
- ❖ acrylic paints in red, white and black
- ❖ black markers or crayons
- ❖ clear acrylic spray
- ❖ wood glue

For each child—
- ❖ sandpaper

Standard Supplies
- ❖ ruler
- ❖ white card stock
- ❖ newspaper
- ❖ shallow containers
- ❖ paintbrushes
- ❖ scissors

DAY ONE
Preparation

Saw boards into two 6-inch (15-cm) squares for each child. Saw two top corners off of each square to make barn end pieces (sketch a). Saw additional boards into one 4x6-inch (10x15-cm) rectangle for each child to make slider piece. Saw two 12-inch (30.5-cm) lengths of dowel for each child. Drill two ½-inch (1.3-cm) holes in each barn end piece, 1 inch (2.5 cm) from bottom and 3 inches (7.5 cm) apart (sketch b). Drill two ⅝-inch (1.6-cm) holes in each slider piece, corresponding to holes in end pieces (sketch c). Photocopy onto card stock two copies of Cow Pattern for each child. Cover work area with newspaper. Pour paints into shallow containers.

Instruct each child in the following procedures:

- Use sandpaper to smooth rough edges on all wood pieces.
- Paint barn and rectangle pieces red.
- Cut out card-stock cows. Use marker to draw spots and eyes on cow cutouts.
- Use black and white paint to decorate barn pieces to look like a barn (sketch d). Allow paint to dry.

DAY TWO
Preparation

In a well-ventilated area, spray all wood pieces with clear acrylic spray.

Instruct each child in the following procedures:

- Glue cow cutouts securely to either side of wood rectangle piece, above the holes.
- Put glue on one end of each dowel and place into drilled holes of one barn end piece. Slide cow slider piece onto dowels. Glue opposite ends of dowels into drilled holes of second barn end piece (sketch d).
- At home, place books on shelf. Slide cow next to books to keep them upright.

Enrichment Idea

Children paint their own designs on slider pieces, instead of using Cow Pattern.

The Farm Report

What book have you read recently? What is one thing you learned from the book? We can learn lots of things from books. The Bible is the most important book you can read. What can you learn from the Bible? In the Bible, we can learn about good qualities that God helps us grow in our lives. In Galatians 5:22, these good things are called the fruit of the Spirit. The Bible tells us that *the fruit of the Spirit is love, joy, peace, patience, kindness, goodness, faithfulness, gentleness and self-control* (Galatians 5:22-23). You can keep your Bible on your Barn Bookshelf and read it often to help you grow!

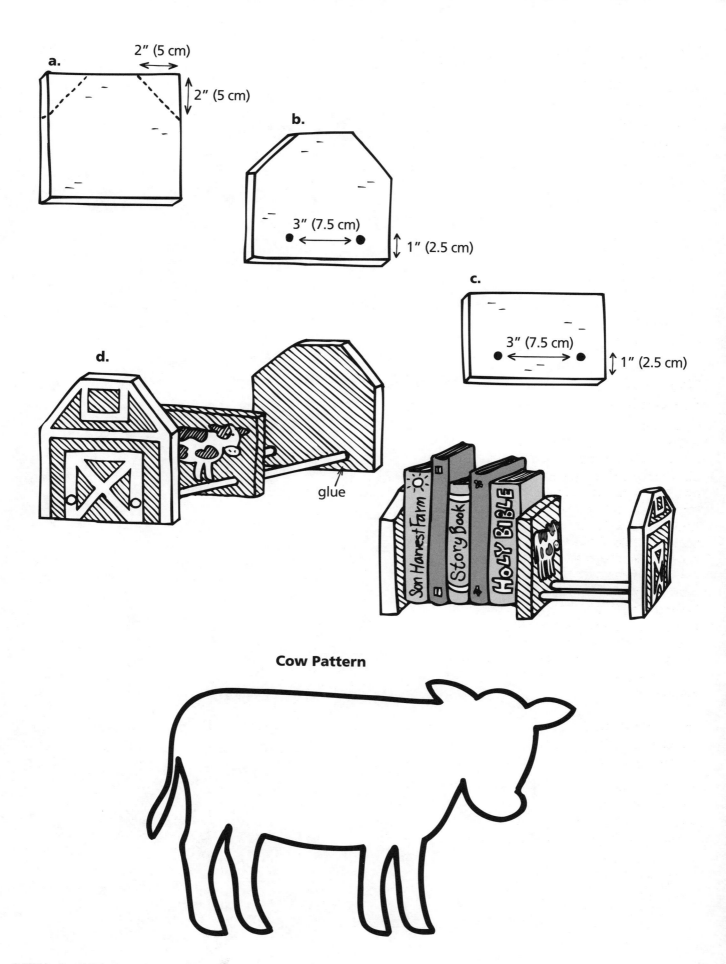

a.

2" (5 cm)

2" (5 cm)

b.

3" (7.5 cm)

1" (2.5 cm)

c.

3" (7.5 cm)

1" (2.5 cm)

d.

glue

Son Harvest Farm

Story Book

HOLY BIBLE

Cow Pattern

Section Four
Bonus Pages

Henrietta Chicken Glove Puppet
Use the instructions and patterns for Henrietta puppet to make your own glove puppet for prekindergarten and kindergarten children to enjoy.

Fruit Patterns
Use these simple fruit patterns for several crafts in this book. Or photocopy and enlarge them onto appropriate colors of construction paper and cut out for an easy room decoration.

Seed Packet Patterns
Photocopy the Seed Packet Patterns onto card stock. Children cut, color, fold and glue to make seed packets that represent five of the fruit of the Spirit. Children may use them to make several crafts in this book.

Coloring Pages

Prekindergarten and Kindergarten Coloring Pages
These large simple pictures are designed for the littlest artists in your program. Each page also contains a simple Bible verse.

Bible Memory Verse Coloring Pages
Use these fun-to-color designs to reinforce Bible memory verses. There are five pages for younger elementary children and five for older elementary children.

Fruit of the Spirit Coloring Pages
These bold designs will help kids remember the first five fruit of the Spirit. Use these reproducible coloring pages in any of the following ways:

❖ Use as awards for children who memorize the Bible verse. They may take them home to color and display.

❖ Photocopy a set of coloring pages for each student. Cover with a folded sheet of construction paper and staple to make a coloring book.

❖ Use in class for transition times or for students who finish an activity ahead of other students.

❖ Play a coloring game. Place a variety of markers on the table. Recite the verse together. Then each student may choose a marker and use it to color on his or her design for one minute. When time is up, students put markers down and repeat verse together again. Students then choose another marker and color for one minute. Repeat process until coloring is completed or students tire of activity.

❖ Customize any coloring page by covering the Bible verse with white paper and printing another verse or saying in its place before you photocopy.

Student Certificates and Awards
The awards and certificates on the following pages may be personalized for various uses. Just follow these simple procedures:

1. Tear out certificate, and print the name of your program on the appropriate line.
2. Photocopy as many copies of certificate as needed.
3. Print each child's certificate with his or her name (and achievement when appropriate).

Sticker Posters
1. Photocopy a sticker poster for each student.
2. After students color posters, attach them to a wall or bulletin board.
3. Have students add stickers to their posters each day as they arrive. Or use stickers as rewards for reciting Bible memory verses, being helpful or completing assignments.

Henrietta Chicken Glove Puppet

Materials

❖ Chicken Puppet Patterns
❖ one white cotton gardening glove
❖ 3-inch (7.5-cm) Styrofoam ball
❖ one red bumpy chenille wire
❖ tan felt
❖ two large wiggle eyes

Optional—
❖ purchased feathers
❖ fiberfill stuffing

Standard Supplies

❖ scissors
❖ craft glue

Instructions:

• Use scissors to make a hole in Styrofoam ball large enough for your thumb. The hole will be the bottom of puppet's head (sketch a).

• Cut one bump from chenille wire. (Leave remaining three bumps intact.) Fold chenille bump in half at center for a beak and glue onto head, pushing it slightly into Styrofoam ball (sketch a). Trim any sharp ends.

• Glue wiggle eyes onto head, just above beak (sketch a).

• Bend remaining three bumps of chenille wire for a comb as shown in sketch b. Glue comb to head, pushing wire slightly into Styrofoam (sketch c).

• Trace Tail Feather Pattern onto tan felt and cut out eight feathers. (Optional: Instead of using Tail Feather and Wing Patterns, glue real feathers onto glove for tail and wings.)

• Trace Wing Pattern onto tan felt and cut out two wings.

• Glue one felt feather to each side of each finger of glove (sketch c). Glue one wing to each side of glove (sketch c). Let dry.

• Insert hand into glove and glue Styrofoam ball onto glove thumb (sketch c). Allow to dry at least two minutes before removing hand from glove. (Optional: With hand inside puppet, stuff both sides of glove with fiberfill for a fatter chicken.)

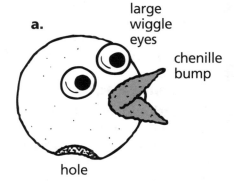

a. large wiggle eyes

chenille bump

hole

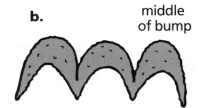

b. middle of bump

Chicken Puppet Patterns

Tail Feather
Cut eight.

Wing
Cut two.

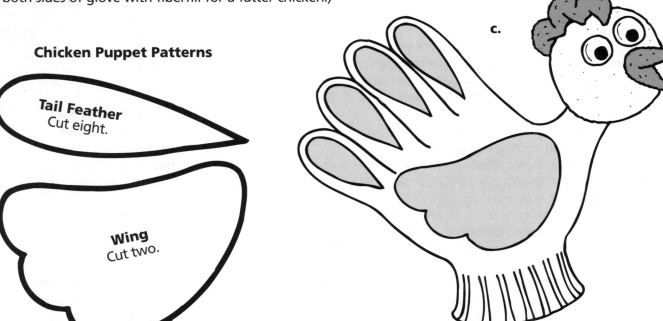

c.

Fruit Patterns

Seed Packet Patterns

Color and cut out seed packet patterns. Fold packet patterns along all dashed lines to make an envelope (see sketches). Glue side and bottom tabs to secure.

Use seed packets to make the seed packet crafts found in this book (pp. 36, 37 and 51). Or tuck a note or small card, real seeds, stickers or a small gift inside a seed packet to give to someone.

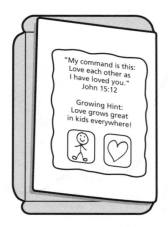  

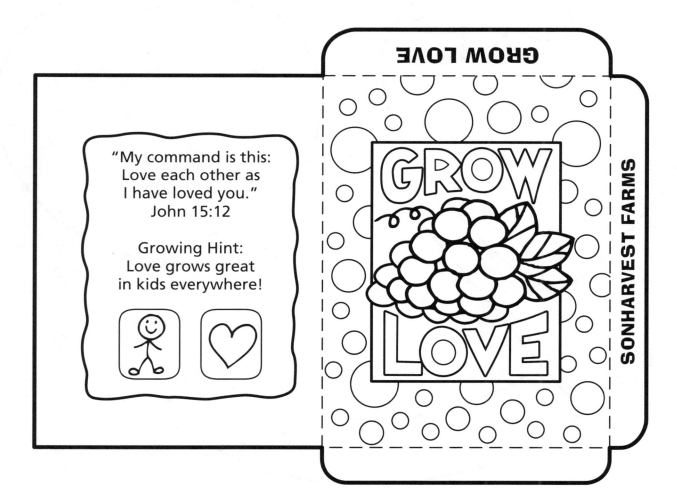

SPROUT JOY

"The Lord has done great things for us, and we are filled with joy." Psalm 126:3

Growing Hint: Joy sprouts best when you're thankful!

SONHARVEST FARMS

PLANT PEACE

"My peace I give you. . . . Do not let your hearts be troubled and do not be afraid." John 14:27

Growing Hint: You can plant peace in all kinds of weather!

SONHARVEST FARMS

PRODUCE PATIENCE

"Be completely humble and gentle; be patient, bearing with one another in love."
Ephesians 4:2

Growing Hint: Give patience time to grow!

SONHARVEST FARMS

PICK KINDNESS

"Always try to be kind to each other and to everyone else."
1 Thessalonians 5:15

Growing Hint: Plant kindness where it's least expected!

SONHARVEST FARMS

"[Jesus said,] 'Love each other as I have loved you.'" John 15:12

Prekindergarten/Kindergarten Coloring Page 1

"The Lord
gives us joy."
(See Psalm 126:3.)

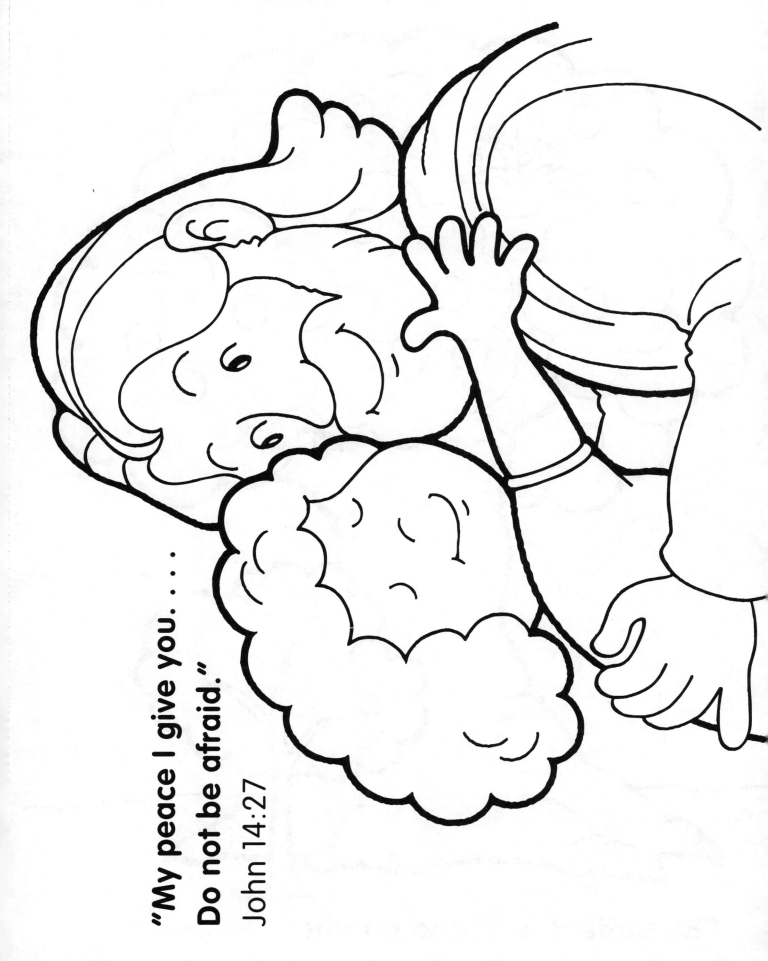

"My peace I give you. . . . . . Do not be afraid."

John 14:27

Prekindergarten/Kindergarten Coloring Page 3

"Be patient with one another." (See Ephesians 4:2.)

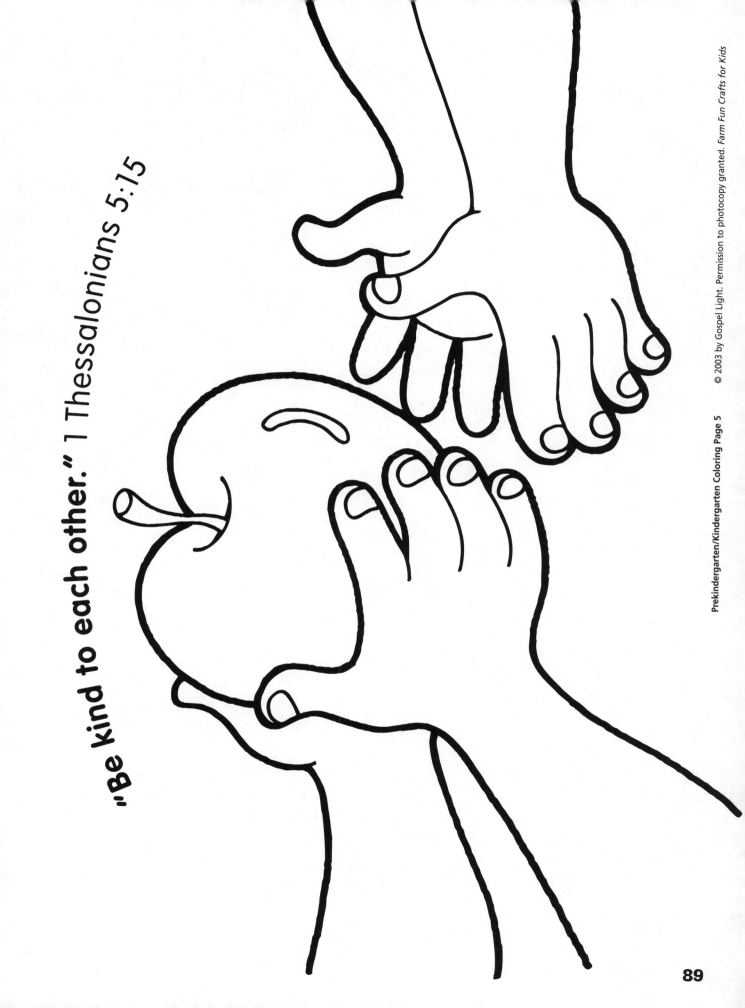

"Be kind to each other." 1 Thessalonians 5:15

"[Jesus said,] 'My command is this: Love each other as I have loved you.'"
John 15:12

Younger Elementary Coloring Page 1

"The Lord has done great things for us, and we are filled with joy." Psalm 126:3

Younger Elementary Coloring Page 2   © 2003 by Gospel Light. Permission to photocopy granted. *Farm Fun Crafts for Kids*

"My peace I give you. . . . . Do not let your hearts be troubled and do not be afraid."

John 14:27

Younger Elementary Coloring Page 3

"Be completely humble and gentle; be patient." Ephesians 4:2

 Younger Elementary Coloring Page 4   © 2003 by Gospel Light. Permission to photocopy granted. *Farm Fun Crafts for Kids*

"Always try to be kind to each other and to everyone else." 1 Thessalonians 5:15

Jesus said, "My command is this: Love each other as I have loved you." John 15:12

Older Elementary Coloring Page 1

"The Lord has done great things for us, and we are filled with joy."
Psalm 126:3

Older Elementary Coloring Page 2 © 2003 by Gospel Light. Permission to photocopy granted. *Farm Fun Crafts for Kids*

"My peace I give you. . . . . Do not let your hearts be troubled and do not be afraid." John 14:27

"Be completely humble and gentle; be patient, bearing with one another in love." Ephesians 4:2

"Always try to be kind to each other and to everyone else." 1 Thessalonians 5:15

101

Fruit of the Spirit Coloring Page 1   **103**

Fruit of the Spirit Coloring Page 2 © 2003 by Gospel Light. Permission to photocopy granted. *Farm Fun Crafts for Kids*

Fruit of the Spirit Coloring Page 3

PRODUCE

PATIENCE

Fruit of the Spirit Coloring Page 4

Fruit of the Spirit Coloring Page 5   **107**

Kind Friend Award

_____

showed kindness at

_____

Visitor Award

_____ ,

we're glad you came to

_____ .

It would be a **JOY** to have you back!

_____,

thanks for pitchin' in at

_____

_____

Blue Ribbon

memorized all the
Bible Memory Verses at

Faithful Farmer Award

_____

_____

_____

Thanks for nurturing
God's little seedlings!

_____

showed the fruit of the Spirit by

_____

Index of Crafts